THE CULT OF THE
BIG RIGS
AND THE LIFE OF THE LONG HAUL TRUCKER

THE CULT OF THE

BIG RIGS

AND THE LIFE OF THE LONG HAUL TRUCKER

by Graeme Ewens and Michael Ellis

Contents

A QUARTO BOOK
Published by Blue Rig, 33 Parkfield Avenue,
Northolt. Middlesex. England.

ISBN 0—9505921—0—2
First published 1977
Reprinted 1978
© Copyright 1977 Quarto Limited
This book was designed and produced by Quarto,
666 Fifth Avenue, New York, N.Y. 10019.

Written by Graeme Ewens. Devised by Michael Ellis
and Graeme Ewens. Original photography by John
Mason (full credits page 192). Jacket by Andrew
Holmes. Design by Michael Ellis. Text editor David
Hardy. Editorial director Michael Jackson.

Phototypeset in Britain by Filmtype Services Limited,
Scarborough, Yorkshire.
Printed in Hong Kong.
by Leefung Asco Printers Ltd.

A Living Legend

The American trucker

The guy who drives a long haul truck has always been of a special breed, yet to millions of city dwellers, whose lives are rarely crossed by a major highway, this vital member of the community might just as well live in another world. Only recently has the rest of the population started to come somewhere near understanding the complexity and self-containment of that world of rolling wheels and diesel smoke. Over the last decade roughly coinciding with the completion of the Interstate Highway System, the status of the trucker has risen, along with his standard of living. The stereotype, blue-collared, uniform-capped figure, with greasy fingers and a pot belly is a thing of the past. He has been replaced by a new-look, slimline character in a fancy shirt and western boots, whose rig is the pride of the highway, whose road judgment is widely respected, and whose lifestyle is increasingly envied. This is the independent trucker of today.

Any professional who has to earn his living surrounded by virtually untrained and unpredictable amateurs, who often use unsafe and inferior equipment, deserves to be respected, if not actually regarded as a hero. Doing that job in the varying, and often extreme conditions found on the highways of this land, demands nothing less.

But where the independents really rise above the rest to become living legends is when they invest so much of their lives in a fancy machine which symbolically asserts their individuality, and in practice enables them to challenge the world of big business – with the ultimate aim of freedom.

The United States is one of the largest, and certainly the most mobile, of nations.

This goes some way to explaining the special status and importance of the trucker in the 20th century. He operates in a closed community, recognized by the rest of the population, but almost impenetrable. We see the trucker at work, high up in his lofty cab; occasionally, we see him eating at the 'truckers only' counter; we may also see him in a ditch, or curse him when we are behind him on a steep, narrow grade.

Naturally, he looks pretty much like anyone else, although there are distinguishing marks: the way he rubs his eyes, the lines around them, the baggy, elephant-assed seat of his jeans, the sole of the right boot that is worn thin, and the way he is always trying to stretch his back. Conversation with him would reveal some of the more permanent effects of road fever: the broken homes, the alienation, the boredom, the ulcers, kidney trouble, heart disease, mental and physical fatigue which overshadow his freewheeling existence.

To the rest of us, however, the trucker is just a man sitting six feet above the ground, looking at the world from his awesome and exciting rig. He can see for miles over the country, and will probably still be rolling on his way long after the rest of us are safely tucked up in bed. There is a sense of urgency in the way those big rigs roll, so businesslike that the ordinary four-door family car looks ridiculous in its company. Once out of the city limits, with the great open highway ahead, he really comes into his own. He can then wind up his diesel to a comfortable speed, check out the road ahead on his CB radio, settle back in his air-ride seat, and point the truck between the ditches for as long as his stamina will permit. As he cuts across country, trying

America's independent truckers (left) haul much of the nation's freight. They have long been considered Knights of the Road, and are fast approaching the status of folk heroes.

7

to make ground on a continually retreating horizon, he becomes one with his vehicle. Regardless of his actual cargo, he is also carrying the dreams that built a nation.

Traditionally, the United States has depended on the mobility of its people. This extends from the earliest settlers, landing in the east, and those of them who began the long and historic journey west. A land of true opportunity awaited them, but there was a 1,000-mile strip of prairie, rivers, mountains and desert between them and the Pacific Ocean. To people who had already come halfway around the globe looking for a better life, another 2,000 miles or so was not likely to make much difference. However, many of the early trailblazers were not of this stock at all; there were criminals, entrepreneurs, wild men and loners, in addition to many who departed from the European homes with the simple desire to indulge a taste for adventure. Out there, beyond the edge of the wilderness, conditions were hard, and even the well-

Following the white line through Arizona (over page). When the going is easy those eighteen-wheelers run pretty straight and truckers have time to wave back (below and right).

Whatever he's hauling, through whatever kind of country, the truck-driver is master of the highways. In spite of modern technological developments, the truckers of 1949 (above) and 1977 (right and opposite) have many problems in common.

traveled wagon train routes remained rugged long after the railroad had begun the taming process.

It was obvious that so vast a country would not be tamed and settled within a single generation, and mobility was essential. Along with the benefits of industrialization, the new technologies of the machine age brought far greater freedom to move, and the opportunity for the most timid of souls to try their luck in a new environment. Economic slumps motivated many families to pack up their worldly goods and head into the sunset in search of the good life.

The long haul truckers of today are the spiritual descendants of these people. Many drivers come from a long line of truckers, for many children see the open road as a place of romance and adventure, even if it did in many cases cost daddy his wife, or even his life. Once the son of a trucker has been on a trip with his father, and has marveled at the sights,

The closest most people ever get to a semi truck is when they are overtaken on the highway. When a big rig fills the rear view mirror, how many car drivers spare a thought for the truckers who supply the country's needs.

sounds and smells of faraway states, he will have that bug in his blood, and there is little anyone can do to prevent it from growing into an irresistible urge to follow that white line. However, the closest most of us will ever get to a big 18-wheeler is when they fill the windows of the family sedan. City folks will stop to gaze at his out-of-state plates – all 10 of them, and they will usually return the wave of the man up there behind the wheel.

Truckers themselves feel that every once in a while, they are singled out as public enemies, mostly by the local media which is either short of scapegoats, or has been unfairly primed by anti-trucker police or oppressive legislative action. The state of Ohio, in particular, has been seen by many to wage a private battle against the truckers, with the law enforcement agencies at the center of the action. Before the overall 50mph limit, Ohio was notorious for its harsh application of speed regulations. Local communities can easily be whipped up by carefully-presented police accident reports supplied by local newspapers. The harm done by just one such story more than cancels out the many Good Citizenship awards, and the educational work

INFERIOR BRAKE BLOCKS SELDOM GIVE YOU A SECOND CHANCE

Every truck on our highways and city streets today that's equipped with inferior brake blocks is an accident waiting to happen! Inferior blocks can't be depended upon when the driver really needs them. And usually, when their inadequate performance is discovered, it's too late.

POOR INVESTMENT. Inferior blocks are a bad investment in another way, too. They cost more in the long run than quality blocks. (And sometimes they cost as much to buy.) They cost more per month and per mile—force your trucks into the garage for block replacement more often.

It's a cinch no truck operator would intentionally put unsafe, inferior blocks on his trucks. But the catch is, how do you know whether you're buying inferior blocks or quality blocks? No one except experienced brake block engineers can evaluate the quality of block material. Looking at the material and feeling it offers no clue to its true worth. In fact, many inferior blocks are put on the market and sold with both the wholesaler and truck operator believing they're the best money can buy!

SAFETY LAST. These blocks are turned out with crude methods and equipment and with no regard for their ultimate performance in the field. It's safety last and profit first with the men who make them . . . as long as the stuff sells, who cares what it's made of or how it's made? Well, we care!

NAME YOUR BRAND. Bendix—and the several other manufacturers of top quality brake lining—would like to get junky, unsafe blocks off the market once and for all. Every truck operator, mechanic and brake block wholesaler can help by specifying blocks by *name*—Bendix or the name of any other top-quality block manufacturer. Don't let the guy who's selling them to you say, "This stuff is just as good, and it'll save you a little dough". Know what you're buying and who you're buying it from. That way you'll know you're getting longer service life—and maximum safety, too.

46

COMMERCIAL CAR JOURNAL, June, 1958

done by trucking organizations all over the country.

The National Safety Council's records show that since the 1940s, when trucks averaged 57 accidents per million miles, the rate has plunged, In 1974, the rate was only 13 accidents per million miles, and it is continuing to drop, in spite of the fact that there are many more heavy trucks, driving many more miles than there were 30 years ago.

These trucks run through all weathers, every day of the year. On a clear night, with a straight and level road, the running might be easy, there are other times, when the weather is at its foulest, when trucking is a deadly serious business. Times when there is suddenly no air in the brakes, or when they are overheated and starting to burn, when the fog comes sweeping down, when the whole rig skates sideways across black ice, when the front wheel blows out, when the road is slicked by a thousand frogs. In addition

As the song says 'There ain't no easy run'. Truck drivers have to be alert to all the hazards of the road (right). They keep an eye on their own tails with big, flat 'West Coast' mirrors (opposite).

to these there are high winds, twisters and snowstorms, all part of the pattern of hazards a trucker could face on just about any working day.

Of course, there are bad or irresponsible truck drivers, but the majority stick to the unwritten code that dictates that it is better for a driver to put his vehicle off the road than run into a passenger car. Those who have been assisted by a trucker at a breakdown or accident, regard these men as the Kings of the Road. Whether they are stranded way out in the desert with a burst radiator, or in a blizzard without chains, or just on the road with a flat tire, the first vehicle to stop with an offer of help will probably be a truck. This is now accepted as a fact by the majority of road-users, most of whom have never needed aid, or would never stop to consider what a debt they, as consumers, owed to the trucker. In fact, about the most common piece of highway lore among the ordinary motor-

ist is that the trucker is the man who knows all the best places to eat.

To most people, he is, above all, thought of as an individual. For one thing, he has mastery over a machine, possibly one of the few dragons left to slay in this day and age. Any hot rodder, car freak, vanner, or four-wheel driver can put his all into one little two-axle baby. However, take it out on the highway and, apart from sheer speed, it would be shamed out of sight by a big rig in full dress. Indeed, even in terms of speed, there are few autos which can cruise at 100mph for 1,000 miles, like a 400 or 500hp semi, given an open road, clean of weigh stations and bears.

The chrome and custom paint jobs – known as gingerbread or full dress – give the rigs an identity that rubs off on the driver. They are, perhaps, the most extreme of personal body extensions. Not only do they protect and provide for their master-occupant, they allow him

Truckers may live in a different world (above), but they retain a reputation for aiding motorists in distress (left) which goes back to the earliest days of transport.

The double sleeper Kenworth (preceding page) has the largest cab made, and is popular with owner operators. Another popular custom-built truck is the Peterbilt (above and right).

to live in a style of personal comfort and luxury that only a five-star hotel could match. With such a close relationship between truck and trucker, it's hardly surprising that most of the independents take a great pride in maintaining the vehicle's appearance and performance.

The loners do not, of course, represent more than a part of the overall scene. Although the company men blaze a somewhat less spectacular trail, they are just as closely involved with their workhorse vehicles. While they probably admire the appearance of a newly-washed and sparkling custom Pete or Kenworth, and envy the celebrity status of the drivers, company men do have their own thing going for them. They have guaranteed wages and conditions which preclude working

over the agreed hours. A senior driver for a company like Roadway or Consolidated Freightways will make good money, and see his wife and kids a lot more than the independent. However, he is not free in the sense that the independent would understand. It is the freedom from Boss Man and clock-punching that the owner-operator seeks. Like most things in life, it comes at a price. All the way down the line, the independent will run into bureaucratic hassles, and this will apply whichever way he has decided to run his truck.

Whether he drives himself, or employs a friend or relative – many owner-operators have more than one truck – there are two ways in which he can put the rig to work. He can haul regulated freight only if he obtains the required permits, so the most common solution is to lease the tractor and services to a regulated carrier. About a third of all interstate trucking is conducted on this basis. If leased to such a company, the tractor would probably have to be painted in the company's livery, and would pull a com-

If driving a company truck is too much like a regular job (left), a trucker can haul for himself or lease his truck and services to a larger organization (above).

pany trailer. Almost all the major van lines in the United States use owner-operators. Freight lines, on the other hand, almost always operate their own trucks. When a trucker is leased to a company, he will be paid either on a percentage basis, or on a mileage rate. If he is fortunate enough to gross $2,000 or $3,000 a week, it must be remembered that all his expenses, including the truck repayments, insurance, tax and servicing, must come out of this.

Some commodities are exempt from Interstate Commerce Commission regu-

lations, and these can be hauled by anyone with the equipment, and broker to provide the loads. The difference between exempt and non-exempt commodities is sometime obscure, but the categories are occasionally reviewed. For instance, in 1977, citrus fruit was exempt, but bananas were not; frozen chicken dinners were exempt, but beef dinners were not.

One type of load which is generally exempt, and which is the mainstay of the independent hauler, is agricultural produce. Produce haulers invariably have

A produce-hauler piles on the coal through Mississippi (preceding page). This page: Once a guy has a tractor (above) he must decide on his line of business. The double trailers on the left are for hauling livestock.

Opening the roads

The old plank road (top left) was laid in Oregon around 1910. Planks were preferable to dirt roads, especially when it rained. The oiling and spreading of 'hot stuff' is being done some ten years later. Rowena Loops on the Columbia River Highway (middle right) was also built around 1920. By the 1950s complex interchanges (bottom left) were being built everywhere, and by the 1970s highways ran smooth and simple.

their own trailers, which must be refrigerated. However, even the different fruits and vegetables need to be kept at different temperatures.

Once the novice trucker has his rig, sorted out a load and got the paperwork licked, he joins a band of true Americans as a small businessman. The attractions are many, but, increasingly, the cry is heard from the owner-operators, that the only heroism now involved is in fighting bureaucracy. Freight lines are becoming more and more monopolistic. The independents now see themselves as champions of individual freedom, fighting to retain their right to work.

A Diamond Reo driver goes lickety-spit through the Texas rain (above), delivering the goods and keeping alive the legend.

The Rigs

From pioneer days to the present time

The first purpose-built gasoline truck was produced in 1896 at the Daimler Benz factory in Germany. By the turn of the century, the company – later to be known as Mercedes Benz – were turning out trucks capable of carrying a five-ton payload.

In America, the horse was still the most favored means of transportation, and the sight of the early automobiles gave horse and buggy drivers much amusement. They found no reason to believe that they were about to be over-taken by one of the greatest revolutions in history. The autos of this age were small and temperamental and, although some vehicles were converted for load-carrying, many people thought it was all a passing fashion. However, some big cities had already anticipated what was to come by paving the roads for the electric buggies which were already run-ning local deliveries.

These electric vehicles were, of course, limited to short journeys between battery charge-ups, and their speeds were no faster than those of the horses. They did, however, have the great advantage of not needing to be fed and bedded down, and by the start of the 20th century they were a common sight on city streets, carrying milk, bread and groceries.

While the early internal combustion engine had only enough power to pull a lightweight car with a human cargo, the steam engine had already been adapted to pull vehicles. Apart from its obvious use as a railroad locomotive, the steam engine had long been a tool of fire departments. At first, they used it to power the pumps which were pulled by horses. Later, companies such as Ward La France discovered the great truth that steam could actually propel the vehicle itself much faster than a team of horses could. Similar developments were also taking place among the manufac-turers of farm machinery, where steam engines began to work the threshing and harvesting machines.

With these heavy and specialized machines able to propel themselves, it seemed logical to many people that steam should transport heavy loads. Several companies went into business selling steam trucks, but only a few survived after World War One. Close on the heels of these pioneer trucks was the rapidly-developing gasoline engine. By 1905, several types of gasoline-powered truck were available.

Most of these vehicles were converted autos, which were in turn little more than converted horse buggies. In 1903, Mack had taken things a step further with the introduction of a four-cylinder gasoline bus, and in the same year the Swiss firm of Saurer was exporting five-ton trucks to the United States. Two years later, competition became more heated when Mack and Studebaker also announced their own five-ton trucks. These vehicles had no cabs, the driver sat on a wooden

This old Virginia country road was typical of the early state highway systems (left). The Saurer 'Pioneer Freighter' (below) is seen crossing a railroad track on its important Transcontinental journey.

GMC TRUCKS

bench, which was positioned directly above the front axle, with the exposed steering column running down between his legs. The wheels were of the wooden, carriage type, with a hard rubber strip to protect the rim. The driver's comfort was not seriously considered. Leaf springs similar to those seen today were used, but their purpose was merely to cushion the blows to the load and vehicle; again, they were not intended as a concession to the man behind the wheel.

Country people remained scornful of these new-fangled machines, but they were quickly catching on in the urban areas. By 1908, Mack was even producing a dump body for the construction industry. The corporation was also standardizing production methods and introducing dual rear tires and thicker rubber on its heavy-duty vehicles. Although the Mack Brothers had got off to a flying start with their New York factory, they certainly did not have things all their own way. In 1907, a merger between two makers of agricultural machinery led to

the formation of the International Harvester company, who soon began to produce motor trucks. Two years later, White Brothers built a gasoline truck and, in Michigan, both Rapid Motor Vehicles and Reliance Motor Truck were in production.

In 1910, Rapid sent a vehicle on a 3,000-mile demonstration run, starting and finishing at the company's Detroit factory. However, all the prestige thus gained was soon forgotten, for two years later Rapid and Reliance were swallowed up by General Motors, which already controlled Buick, Cadillac and Olds. Hewitt was another independent truck manufacturer to win only short-lived success. In 1909, the company was using aluminium crankcases and pressed steel frames to build the biggest truck of its time which, thanks to upgraded springs and wheels, could transport a 10-ton payload. Only two years later, Hewitt's name also disappeared when the company merged with Mack.

Saurer had been doing well in the

American market and, in 1911, a company was set up to build trucks under licence in the United States. As part of an ambitious sales drive, Saurer sent a truck on the first ever transcontinental trip. Called the Pioneer Freighter, the truck completed the journey in two stages. The first leg was westwards from Denver to San Francisco, and it proved to be the hardest ever undertaken by a truck. It took three months to get the Pioneer over the mountains and through the desert, where there were often no roads at all. They frequently took to the railroad tracks when the road disappeared, or was too rough for the vehicle. The journey across New Mexico took almost a month. The truck was carrying a cargo of timber, which was used for bridging gullies.

After being shipped back to Colorado, the Saurer was then driven east to Chicago and New York, where it arrived after clocking more than 5,000 miles, including diversions and demonstration runs. This trailblazing achievement did not save American Saurer from merger with the expanding Mack empire only two years later.

Trucking was really beginning to grow up fast and in 1916, a husband and wife and their child set out in a 1½-ton GMC truck to travel from Seattle to New York, along the new National Park Highway, which was little more than a network of dirt roads. Their total travel time was 31 days, and the following year the husband and wife made the return trip to Seattle. Also in 1917, a Packard truck ran 750 miles from Akron, Ohio, to Boston, Mass. This 19-day trip was sponsored by Goodyear, who were showing off the advantages of their pneumatic tires.

However, not everything was happening in the East. In 1916, a company in Portland, Oregon, produced the first Gersix custom-built truck. This six-cylinder conventional, with full electrical equipment, took one month to build, and was sold for $4,000 – twice the price of a Mack. It was the start of the West Coast custom-building tradition and,

By 1916 demonstration runs were almost commonplace. Mr and Mrs William Warwick deliver the first Transcontinental shipment (left). The Packard used on the Goodyear run (above) took 19 days to make 750 miles over inferior roads and bridges.

six years later, the company changed its name to Kenworth.

Trucks really began to come into their own in the first World War. The AC Mack, which was designed by Hewitt before the merger, was destined to become a most important wartime vehicle. It was the first production truck to be built with a steel cab and optional roof. It was ordered in thousands by the Allied forces in Europe. The British press reported that the pugnacious styling of the steel hood had caused the British troops to christen it the Bulldog Mack. The success of this chain-driven model did wonders for the Mack reputation and the bulldog was quickly adopted the company symbol.

The necessary increase in production

during the war years stimulated the American economy and, with it, the truck-building industry. A boom in construction meant that contractors were in the market for heavy duty vehicles. Manufacturers also needed them for essential transportation and, when Federal Aid was made available for the first major road-building program, trucks were at last given somewhere to run. One of the early results of that scheme was the Lincoln Highway. In 1919, this road carried Eisenhower's Transcontinental army convoy from Washington DC to San Francisco.

Improved road conditions were making trucking a far more efficient business. Truck-trailer combinations, and semi-trailer outfits were finding favor in many

parts of the country, especially where weight restrictions were already being imposed. Top manufacturers, such as Ford, International, GMC, White and Mack, were operating production lines. Smaller companies, including the likes of Reo, Packard, and Diamond T, were turning out light- and medium-weight trucks, while in Wisconsin, Oshkosh and FWD were building heavy duty special equipment and establishing the high reputation which they still enjoy for tough, off-road vehicles.

The immediate post-war years were not great days for many of the factories. Thousands of war surplus vehicles came onto the market and many people, particularly in the West, still preferred horses. The harsh economic pressures

The AC model Mack was in production from 1915 to 1938. The early trailer model (above) was one of the larger versions of the Bulldog series. The FWD (left) is seen redressing old macadam on Oregon Pacific Highway about 1919. The two Autocars overleaf are shown working in the East at about the same time.

proved too much for many of the early companies, who went out of business.

The new Kenworth company, in its Seattle factory, was busily producing tailor-made vehicles for its West Coast customers. Its policy of giving the operator exactly what he wanted ensured that KW were not among the casualties of this difficult time, and Kenworth is now the major builder of high-priced custom trucks. Driving conditions in the west were a lot tougher than they were back East, and many operators and drivers were critical of Eastern-built trucks. Roads in the western states were generally worse, and the long hauls took the drivers through some of the most extreme conditions, such as desert, or snow-covered mountains. Some of the cabs were, by now, fitted with such luxuries as doors and windows, while transmissions had improved, and much work was being done in developing better braking systems. Brakes still had to be adjusted by hand after every pick-up and delivery, because the balance was affected by the weight distribution.

Vehicles were eccentric, and the drivers' lives eventful. Trucks caught fire while going down the long Western grades, or shuddered to a steaming halt while going uphill, leaving the drivers to leap out and quickly block the wheels. In the winter, drivers were likely to freeze, while the summer would have them roasting in their cabs. Attempts were often made to warm up winter driving by diverting engine heat through holes cut in the wooden floors. One common result of this was that the oil-soaked boards would catch fire after coming into contact with red hot manifolds.

However, the thought of driver comfort was there, and the manufacturers began to include items such as padded seats and electric light. Later, operators were able to specify such things as speedometers, bulb horns and rear-view mirrors. By the 1930s, most trucks were built with proper cabs with opening doors and windows, and drivers were soon building their own sleepers.

Trucking boomed during the depression, when fast delivery of goods was

Two examples of conventional trucks. The 1920s International (right) and the later Kenworth (far right) are obviously built for different jobs. The six-axle KW is typical of West Coast rigs of that time. Many smaller makes such as the Rugby (below) catered to the lightweight end of the market.

DURABILITY — ECONOMY — POWER — SPEED

RUGBY TRUCKS are Engineered *by* Experts to Cut Haulage Costs

The new and finer Rugby Trucks, built by Durant, are products of recognized experts who have studied every business in which transportation is a factor. They are engineered to cut haulage costs to the minimum.

Integral with the 6-cylinder engine is a specially designed truck transmission, with direct drive in high and exceptionally low first-speed gear ratio.

This typifies the mechanical and structural features that distinguish the new Rugby — features vital to dependability and long life, and unobtainable at less than Rugby prices.

DURANT MOTORS, INC., EXPORT DIVISION
1819 WOODWARD AVE., DETROIT, U.S.A.

RUGBY
A GOOD TRUCK — BUILT BY DURANT

seen as a way to save time and money. The railroads suffered as a result, and lost much business that was never recovered.

Length restrictions were introduced in some states during this decade, and this saw a revival of the cabover engine design. Although the earlier rigs were steered from over the engine, the majority of trucks since had been conventionals with long hoods reminiscent of auto styles. The new cabovers enabled longer trailers to be pulled. Twin axles were also introduced to help with weight distribution. The familiar five-axle profile, which is so common now, dates back to those days.

Ever the innovator, the German firm of Benz had been responsible in 1923 for introducing the first diesel engined truck. Diesels had been used in America to power such things as generators, but the

development needed to turn these slow-running motors into efficient automotive engines was not completed in the United States until 1932 when the first Cummins diesel engine was installed in a Kenworth. Diesels are approximately 40 per cent more efficient than their gasoline counterparts, because they convert so much more of the fuel which they consume into energy. In addition to this, diesel fuel was at this time only half the price of gas.

The 100hp Cummins may have been the first big diesel engine, but in 1938 Mack came out with a 131hp mill, proclaiming it as the first maker-supplied diesel. In the same year, the first Caterpillar CID series automotive diesel was installed in a tough-looking HUG tractor. The HUG company, founded in 1922, lasted only 20 years, but in that time produced many rugged off-road and

construction trucks for state highway departments. Their over-the-road tractors also contained many advanced design features.

The trucking business really became transformed into an industry when the Motor Carrier Safety Act was passed in 1935. The Interstate Commerce Commission, set up in 1887 to regulate commerce – then including railroads, waterways and pipelines – was made responsible for the issuing of permits, fixing rates, licensing carriers and administering the business of interestate trucking. This period saw the tightening of rules in favor of larger carriers, and it also saw the first serious attempts to produce sophisticated long-haul trucks.

Mack was developing its first real interstate tractor and Kenworth was beginning to offer separate sleeper boxes on the new COEs. Brakes had been improved with the first hydraulic and, later, air-braking systems. Styling was also becoming a factor in truck design. The light and medium markets were very much the biggest, and in the mid-30s most manufacturers restyled their range. Dodge offered some of the sleekest lightweights, and International came out with the streamlined D-line. White also redesigned its range, and saw an immediate jump in sales proving that this policy had been right. Ford, which was selling more trucks than anyone at this time, introduced its first cabover, with its distinctive upright oval grill. All Ford trucks were offered with V8 gasoline engines.

Chevrolet and GMC both had a big slice of the market, although most of their sales were in the light and medium

The International D line series
was made from 1937 to 1940, and
reflected the auto styling of the
time. Note the sand boxes
forward of the drive wheels on
this medium-weight semi.

ranges. Diamond T produced a cabover in 1938, and Federal offered drivers of its rigs a factory-installed chrome bumper. Most factories were by now supplying road tractors with a range of engine, transmission and rear axle combinations. Although Mack, Ford, GMC and International still make their own power trains, most makers continue to offer such options and this is the way in which most American trucks are sold.

A public health service study in 1940 led to the introduction of regulations limiting truckers to a 10-hour driving day. The demand was there for sleeper cab versions of the most popular trucks, and the manufacturers were quick to supply them, although just about every factory was occupied with the mass production of army specification soft-skin vehicles for the war in Europe.

Eisenhower had learned from the previous world war the enormous benefits of a motorized army, and in the years from 1939 to 1945, American truck-builders produced and shipped more than three million soft skin vehicles, including jeeps, and more than 150,000 heavy class trucks, in addition to tanks and mobile guns. Before Lease-Lend in 1941, vehicles for Britain, France and China were shipped and paid for through the usual commercial dealers. When France was occupied, large numbers of vehicles were diverted to Britain.

Most of the medium and heavy-duty trucks provided by the United States had multiple drive axles for the off-highway work necessary in a military advance. The 6 × 4 trucks – those with six wheels, four of which drive – were used for most long haul work. The 6 × 6, with power to

The GMC (above) was home front model offered in the early 1940s. Some manufacturers could bring out new designs, but all were producing for the war effort (right).

all three axles, became the workhorse of the European campaign. This truck was classed as light-heavy and the most common version was the GMC, which became known as the Jimmy. Other models were produced by International, Studebaker, Ford and Diamond T. Larger 6 × 6 trucks in the heavy-heavy class, rolled off the production lines of Autocar and White. In 1944, the Diamond T/M20 was introduced, a 6 × 4 road tractor, designed for the British Army and used as a prime mover or

transporter tractor, and in any number of special equipment versions, one of the most successful being the heavy duty wrecker. Many of these tractors survived the war and remained in Europe, where they can still be seen in use.

These trucks were all conventionals and were often supplied with open cabs, but in the later war years both Autocar and Kenworth produced cabovers. Other manufacturers producing heavy-duty vehicles were Mack, with their 'N' series of right-hand trucks, built for the North

Africa campaign, Brockway, Corbitt, Ward La France, Hercules and Pacific Car. Mack and White produced chain-drive 6 × 6 heavy transports, used to haul supplies from Normandy to the front line. These vehicles were also supplied to Russia through the Lease-Lend program.

Among the super-heavies, Oshkosh, Federal and Dart were building special equipment, and Cook Brothers, in California, produced an 8 × 8 chain drive truck for tactical cross-country operations. With the huge number of vehicles in use, wreckers were in great demand, and they had to be especially tough to handle the conditions found on the battlefield. Holmes alone supplied more than 10,000 lifting units to be used on Federal, Beiderman and Diamond T wreckers, while Sterling and Autocar used Gar Wood cranes and equipment.

Although most manufacturers were producing for the war effort, there was a big increase in the home front work load. The order to domestic carriers, who were vital to the production industries, was a categorical, 'Keep 'em rolling'. Three-axle, or tandem, tractors became more necessary to shift the bigger loads, and sleeper cabs were now commonplace.

As well as making trucks, many companies had turned their facilities over to armaments and airplane production. Kenworth were contracted to make aluminum aircraft components for the Boeing plant in Seattle. This expertise was soon put to use in the design of trucks and engines. In 1941, Cummins installed the world's first aluminum diesel engine in a Kenworth, and three years later, KW unveiled the first extruded aluminum frame. In an effort to produce weight-saving trucks, the company began to replace most of the steel sections with the lighter aluminum. At the same time, Kenworth offered purchasers such internal refinements as heaters and adjustable seats, in addition to luxuries such as sealed beam headlights and improved wipers.

After the war, trucking suffered its first setback. Labor conditions were unsettled, production was slumping, there was no highway rebuilding program and traffic was congested. The public was

On the home front, trucks like this White sleeper cab model helped to keep the economy running. This tractor featured a full complement of lights and mirrors, in addition to a modern-looking air filter.

Consolidated Freightways (right) are the parent company of Freightliner. Their first COE model (lower right) was a success with freight haulers. While many companies were bought and sold, International (below) kept truckin' on.

fast becoming disenchanted with heavy trucks. These metal monsters damaged the roads, slowed traffic even further, and clogged up the cities. Trucking was badly in need of a major boost – and Mack helped to supply it. They had developed a vacuum-assisted auxiliary transmission, operated with one hand. With a new diesel engine as well, they really had something to show off. Proclaiming new trucks for a new age, the Mack Diesel Caravan went on the road, touring the country to bring home the vital message that the new prosperity would largely depend on trucks. This was a big effort at public education and public relations; aided by a series of novelties, including model trucks, Mack's initiative was a success.

In 1947, Consolidated Freightways became the first and to date, the only carrier to set up in the business of building its own tractors. Freightliner Cor-

poration was to build the trucks in Portland and, with the exception of those for Consolidated's own use, the vehicles would be marketed by White. This was the birth of the White Freightliner label. The trucks became popular with large fleet operators and, when the industry reached its big turning point in the 1950s, the demand grew for the utility Freightliner. In 1976, Freightliner began to set up their own sales and distribution service, with the new Powerliners aimed at the owner-operator market.

Many companies were unable to survive the difficult period just after the war, and several more were to lose their independence within the next decade. Kenworth had already been sold to Pacific Car and Foundry, the company which also owns Peterbilt. Brockway was by then controlled by Mack, and the White group absorbed Autocar in 1953, Reo in 1957, and Diamond T a year later.

The Korean war saw another increase in production, but it was swiftly followed by a slump. The fluctuating economy, and its effect on production and transportation, forced many companies to diversify. Some were sold out to firms not involved with trucking at all, while the larger manufacturers took over component making.

Throughout the Fifties and Sixties there was a steady rise in overall freight volume. The emergence of the Interstate Highway network was the beginning of the end for the railroad as a major freight carrier. Improvements were continually being made in all areas of truck production, such as the diesel exhaust brake. This is a butterfly device, which is attached to the exhaust manifold. When closed, it holds back the exhaust and increases engine retardation by up to 50 per cent. Exhaust brakes are particularly useful on fast downgrades and many drivers prefer to employ them all the time, leaving the actual wheel brakes until it is absolutely necessary to use them.

Around this time, the Allison division of General Motors offered the first automatic transmission for over the road trucks, but this development did not really begin to catch on with gear jammers until much later. Other improvements which made a more immediate impression were air suspension drivers' seats, which allow the man at the wheel to more or less float on a column of air, cushioning him from the effects of riding over rough roads. Even well-sprung seats cannot protect truckers from a battering and, until recently, it was common for

Three conventional tractors of the 1950s: A 1951 White (top right) and a 1956 Peterbilt (lower right). Peterbilt was founded on the West Coast in 1939, and built custom trucks. The Brockway 'Huskie' (below) was introduced in 1958, after the Mack merger.

Two Cab-Over-Engine tractors:
The H series Mack (left) was
nicknamed the 'Cherry Picker',
and was produced until 1962. The
White (above) is a 1959 model.

many to suffer from kidney complaints.

The design of long-haul trucks did not change more than once every decade and there are still many 1950s rigs rolling the highways today. It is not uncommon for a truck to clock a million miles. A really enthusiastic owner will often keep on rebuilding his vehicle, so that in the end he may have run something like two or three million miles.

Conventionals have changed very little in appearance over the years. Autocar and Peterbilt, in particular, have maintained the classic lines, with split windscreen and headlamps mounted externally on the radiator frame. More recent models, like the 1970s Diamond Reo Raider and the first Freightliner Conventional have shown some harder edge design features, and the giant companies, such as GMC, International, Ford and Dodge, are displaying more auto-influenced profiles.

Cabovers now look almost indistinguishable from each other, mostly because of internal space considerations, and the simplification of body-building techniques. The 1950s H series Macks, whose height earned them the nickname Cherry Pickers, had a different look, as

Two great names from the recent past

Both Diamond T and Reo were taken over by White in the 1950s, then sold to a private company at the beginning of the 1970s, to emerge as Diamond Reo. Their vehicles, built in Lansing, Mich. were marketed by independent dealers, and aimed at owner operators. They built COE and conventional models, although the latter were most popular with truckers. A new range was introduced in 1974 called the Raider, but the company ceased production two years later after getting into difficulties over a contract for government vehicles.

did the bubble-nose KW, and the low profile Corn Binder, produced by International. GMC came up with a square cut sleeper version of their cabover, and this became known as the Crackerbox. With the growing need for larger radiators, bunks, luggage and equipment lockers, and more leg room and vision up front, cabovers have tended to become more flatfronted. However, many designers have rounded off corners of the generally square profile and angled the windshields.

Every year brings with it new regulations, many of them aimed at the truckers, but many more at the manufacturers. The welcome increase in interest in safety and economy measures has led to vast improvements in over the road tractors. Cabs are now well enough insulated to withstand extreme temperatures, suspensions are more agreeable, and power steering can be had as an option on most rigs. Gauges and early warning sensor systems easily fill the modern day dashboard. Heating, braking, cooling, electrical and power train systems can be monitored by the driver. Add to this the array of quadrophonic eight-tracks, AM/FM radio, CB, television and radar detectors, and it is easy to understand that the present day truck cab bears more resemblance to an aircraft cabin than a road vehicle.

Off-road retirement

The automobile industry may have invented 'planned obsolescence', but the truck-builders are made from tougher stuff. There are still plenty of the classic 1950s trucks to be seen around. Some of them are enjoying a peaceful, if undignified, retirement . . . put out to grass, so to speak. Others are still pulling for the nation. These golden oldies are (clockwise from top left), by Diamond T, Chevrolet, Mack, Autocar and International. The GMC shown on the facing page has been restored, and is doing good work on the West Coast.

The Job

Pulling for the Nation

The modern trucker is the man who delivers the goods all over the nation. To him, trucking is a way of life with rewards far outstripping mere cash in the bank.

This is an age in which human independence in commerce and industry is constantly being eroded. The man at the wheel of a big rig is driving along one of the few remaining escape routes to working dignity. Indeed, his freedom in a regimented society would probably attract more than the occasional twinge of envy from the college graduate with a corporate career mapped out all the way to the executive suite.

A job offering such special satisfaction naturally demands special qualities which would rule out most people. The character who chooses to be out on the highway for weeks at a stretch, for an average annual gross of $40,000, is one of a special breed. However, before the would-be independent trucker can begin to live the legend, there is a great deal more to do than simply getting a truck and heading for the road. The whole business of buying or leasing a truck is in itself far from straightforward and, unlike the average auto-purchaser, the trucker must know exactly what he wants before he pays a call on his friendly neighbourhood dealer.

Trucks are not sold as standard. The policy of American truck manufacturers, since the days of the earliest rigs, has been to provide vehicles to do the job, with special equipment for special functions. Any one model will have so many options on engine, wheelbase, transmission, cab size and type, axles, and frame construction, that there could be more than 1,000 versions of the same vehicle. The difference between an off-highway logging truck and an interstate freight hauler, made by the same company, may not be obvious to the uninitiated, but under a uniform skin they will have little in common.

The demands made on the frame will depend on the kinds of loads hauled, the vehicle's gross weight, and the roads on which it will run. For example, a logging truck will require a frame made of steel rails. The logger will spend its working life on rough terrain and will need a raised exhaust and high-mounted fuel tanks.

The general freight-hauler has different needs. The lighter the tractor, the bigger the payload he can carry. Alternatively, he can fit a slightly larger engine, in which case, he will specify an aluminum frame. Engine size and type depend not only on weights, but also on the kinds of routes involved. Certain engines pull better on steep grades, others are economic fuel consumers in hot desert conditions, or on high altitude runs. Engines vary in power from about 250hp to the big 450 and 600hp V12 diesels.

The trucker's next step is to decide on wheelbase and axle configuration for the tractor. There are two basic tractor designs: The long-nosed, traditional-looking 'conventional' and the flat-fronted 'cabover'. Most new trucks on the market are offered in both guises. A conventional's long nose is an important safety plus. In the event of a crash, the impact will start to be absorbed some eight feet in front of the driver. In addition to this, the geometry of the steering permits the vehicle to ride the highway much more smoothly. The cabover design provides a more convenient driving position, particularly if it is extensively used in city work. Cabs are usually built of aluminum or of the various fiber sandwich materials.

Transmissions, like engines, are generally available for any make of truck. The old-style duplex transmissions, with two-speed boxes and separate shift levers, are still around. However, 13- and 15-speed boxes are the most common today, although automatic transmissions are fast becoming as economical and will eventually make the trucker's life much easier.

Even the modern manuals are not synchromeshed. The range of revs over which a shift can be made is narrow and, when the change is gauged properly, the driver does not need to use the clutch. However, if the right moment is missed, the truck must be brought to a halt in order to get into the right ratio for the road speed. Obviously, this is embarrassing for the trucker – especially on a steep grade, with a line of trucks behind.

The kind of trailer will, of course, depend on the load envisaged. Often the owner-operator will be content to lease from the company for which he is driving. Many companies work on this basis, hiring a trucker and his tractor to pull their own trailers. Most of the major van lines own thousands of special trailers, yet not a single tractor.

Every load has its own characteristics, immediately recognized by the experienced driver. Liquids will slop and, even in modern compartment tankers, the movement of the vehicle will make the

Preceding page: all set to roll. Every type of load has its own characteristics. This Pete (top) has just taken on boards at the LA docks. The three Fords (below) are all designed for different jobs. They are (left) a two-axle COE,(center) a three-axle highway tractor, and (right) a logging version of the same conventional tractor.

liquid surge sideways on the turns and up into the back of the cab when stopping quickly. Frozen carcasses hung from the roof rails of refrigerated trucks also move about, particularly on slow curves. Steel pipes and logs tend to slip forward on heavy braking and, although protective bulkheads are fitted to trucks carrying these loads, the danger is still there. These open loads, carried on flatbed trailers, are held down with chains, but continual shifting of pressure demands constant attention to the bindings. Livestock obviously requires special trailers, and the trucker has to have a special way with animals. It also creates its own problems. Hogs, known to truckers as Go-Go Girls, are particularly fond of moving about as much as they can while on the road. Such livestock needs special attention on long hauls, and there are strict regulations about water and feed.

There are literally hundreds of differing trailer types. Perhaps the most extreme are Michigan doubles, designed to cope with the heavy loads of the local auto industry. These double bottom outfits have as many as 13 axles running the length of the vehicle. Even semi-trailers may have eight axles. Gross weight in Michigan is up to 136,000lbs, and when not running loaded, some axles can be lifted to save on the life of the rubber. California also has design types unfamiliar in the rest of the country. Extra-long tractor wheelbases are common on the West Coast, mainly because they are more stable on the long, hard grades found in those parts.

Other trailer variations across the country include doubles and triples – illegal in most Northern and Eastern states – lowboys, containers, loggers, bulk powder tankers, grain-hoppers, and numerous specialized designs, all carefully planned to provide the most economic and safe means of transporting a particular load.

Life was a great deal simpler in the early days, when the variations were few, and the roads were a lot emptier. The newcomer is not going to find it all quite so easy. Because of the trucking boom at the start of the Seventies, carriers all over the country were crying out for drivers. Advertising campaigns on tele-

In Michigan, they do things their own way. The third trailer axle (above) is lifted to reduce drag. The cost of replacement rubber (below) is offset by heavy gross weights in that state.

Highway patrol

The Wheeler Ridge Inspection station on I-5 is situated north of Los Angeles just before the famous Grapevine. As many as 3000 trucks pass over the scales in a day.

Unlike weigh stations in many states, California's inspection stations, which are administered by the Highway Patrol, are equipped for thorough vehicle inspection.

Annual stickers are issued which are coded and displayed on the truck windshield for identification. If a sticker is out of date or an officer is suspicious of a vehicle as it rolls across the scales, the driver is instructed to pull into an inspection bay.

Inspectors run through the registrations of the vehicles (truck/tractor – trailer – dolly – 2nd trailer) and the driver's log book. A team of mechanics checks out all lamps, mufflers, smog devices, mirrors, wipers, and general equipment. This list of thirty checks even includes the dimensions of the sleeper.

The brake inspection, however, is not included in the mechanical and equipment form. For this there is a separate sheet with 14 points to be checked including gauges, valves, hoses governor, and drums.

The C.H.P. are proud of their thoroughness. The officers on inspection duty are backed up by volumes of regulations, and they consider it appropriate that California, with more vehicles than anywhere in the world, should lead the world in the application of safety standards. Not all truckers agree, particularly those who roll across the scales too overweight or long.

THE TRUCK DRIVER

vision and radio, in magazines and on billboards, urged those with a spirit of adventure to go to trucking school. Hundreds of such schools sprung up all over the country; some were rip-offs, other were responsible establishments, divisions of large, fleet-owning companies, seeking to achieve positive results.

The fees varied, and so did the quality of teaching. Some bogus schools were bold enough to advertise guaranteed employment at the end of the course. No doubt, many pupils ended up bitter and disillusioned. However, many graduates of the reputable schools took to the highways, blissfully unaware of the heavy yoke of responsibility to be dropped around their necks along with owner-operator status.

Cash considerations dictate that most first-time truckers will go to work in a used rig. If the prospective owner-operator wishes to leap straight in with a good Ford, Chevy, or International, he will have to find at least $20,000, and not expect too many frills. If he feels able to chase up some real class, a Pete, or a KW will worry something like $50,000 out of his wallet.

Although most trucks are custom-built, the top class West Coast rigs are actually built by hand, utilizing all the latest aerospace materials. Any manufacturer is capable of turning out a show-

piece truck. All it takes is money. The initial investment is high, but the logic behind it is impeccable. A thoroughbred outfit will come out a whole lot better at trade-in time. Obviously, the specifications of any rig must be laid down to meet the regulations of the states in which it is to operate. If the driver is confining his activities to his home state, the problems are minimized. Interstate driving complicates the operator's life, for his truck must meet the requirements of several departments of transportation, none of whom seem even to be on nodding terms.

Differing gross weight and axle weight limitations from state to state mean that the optimum gross weight nationwide is around 36 tons. However, just so the trucker does not imagine that he is going to get away easily, the maximum length of a semi-trailer rig in some Eastern

Truck-driving schools benefit from publicity campaigns of such bodies as the American Trucking Associations Inc., who do much public relations work on behalf of the trucker (left). Schools can teach a man to put on snow chains but once in the cab, he is on his own.

states is only 55 feet, whereas many states in the West permit lengths of 65, 70, and even 75 feet.

The brave trucker contemplating driving a load right across the nation needs nerves of steel merely to tackle the mountain of forms he will have to fill out. It is the almost endless paperwork that does most to dim the romance of the trucker's existence. Wherever he has to roll that rig, he knows that the driving is only a part of his life, even if it is the part that he enjoys best. A lot of the time up there behind the wheel, he is going to be worrying up a future ulcer because of the red tape awaiting him at the end of the road. Before he even climbs into the cab, he has to be legal. A driver's licence is obviously the first piece of official paper he must possess, and the trucker wishes with all his heart that it ended there. The next things he must seek is a chauffeur's licence, issued by individual states. These are usually issued for three separate classes, decided by gross weight or, as in most cases, the number of axles.

Although federal authorities do not issue driver's licenses, the Interstate Commerce Commission does require certain certificates from anyone wishing to cross a state line. The driver must be over 21, and must carry a Federal Certificate of Road Test, a certificate of written examination, and a medical certificate. Once the individual has collected all his personal papers, he can start to worry about the truck. Motor Carrier Safety Regulations are federal rules that apply to any vehicle used in interstate commerce, although if an individual state has regulations that are

In addition to the license plates (right) trucks must also carry identification stickers for each state they cross (above), and if they have no permit one must be bought for cash (below).

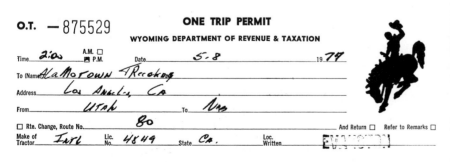

O.T. — 875529

ONE TRIP PERMIT

WYOMING DEPARTMENT OF REVENUE & TAXATION

Time _2:00_ A.M. ☐ P.M. ☑ Date _5-8_ 19 _79_

To (Name) _AlaMotown Trucking_

Address _Los Angeles, Ca_

From _Utah_ To _Nns_

☐ Rte. Change, Route No. _80_ And Return ☐ Refer to Remarks ☐

Make of Tractor _Intl_ Lic. No. _4849_ State _Ca._ Loc. Written _EVANSTON_

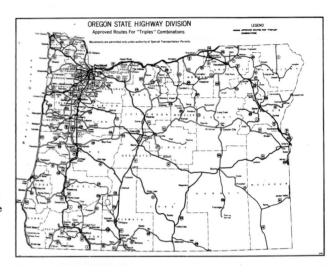

Triple trailer outfits (below) are only allowed to operate in some of the Western states, and then they are restricted to certain roads. Oregon allows lengths of over 100ft.

more severe, then these are the ones to be followed. Until the blanket 55mph limit was imposed, many states had their own differing speed restrictions.

Now the trucker has his rig, a job to go with it, and the pile of paper that makes officialdom smile upon him, he is, at last, ready to get right on down the road. At this stage, he comes face to face with the real red tape tangle that will occupy so much of his time until he says farewell to the highway. Drivers are limited in the number of hours they can spend at the wheel, and they must carry a logbook in which the daily hours are noted: hours driving, hours on duty while not actually driving, hours waiting to be loaded, and hours at rest.

The official limit is 10 hours driving in any one day, but this comes down to 60 hours in any seven days. The well-intentioned reason for logbooks, or comics as many truckers call them, is to reduce the chances of fatigue, which is still the biggest single cause of truck wrecks. Many foreign countries also impose strict limits, some as low as eight hours per day at the wheel. Needless to say, many drivers spend a lot longer on the road. In order to make a decent living,

CB radio has turned the trucker-cop relationship into more of a game than it really is (right). But out on the highway (above) they are both real pros. Preceding page: These tractors will be overhauled, resprayed and sold for $8,000 each.

many owner-operators feel that they must work flat out. It is quite common for the trucker to keep two sets of logbooks, ready to offer up on demand.

The reasons why a trucker might be pulled off the road, and the agencies which are ready to do it to him, are numerous. Nor do they all relate to traffic offences. As well as running a gauntlet of spot checks, and prowling cops all over the country, the interstate trucker is going to run into a weigh station at just about every state line or port of entry. Dodging the scales is an activity central to the world of the trucker, and has been a feature of several songs and truck tales. Before the interstate highway system, when there were fewer trucks around, it was common for overweight and otherwise illegal vehicles to take long detours to avoid weigh-stations. Various departments of transportation were wise to this and introduced moveable scales, which they hauled

around to likely locations. It still happens, but these days the fast roads take most of the traffic. Even so, the spectacular lines of rubber on the highway at the 'Scales Open' sign show that a lot of drivers are taken by surprise.

A special kind of relationship has always existed between truck drivers and bears; it is the rapport of seasoned competitors. The whole thing is rather like an elaborate board game. The trucker has to set off from square one at the best possible speed, and arrive at his destination without being caught. If he succeeds, he is rewarded by the shipper and wins the game outright. The cops are stretched out along the route, and their purpose is to enforce the maze of rules. This is further complicated by local attitudes and tactics. If the cops catch the trucker breaking the rules, he must pay a cash forfeit. If he loses much time as a result, his contract may be at risk, thus sending him financially back to square one.

10-4!
"BEAR IN THE AIR"
POLICE
POLICE
"CHICKEN COOP"
WEIGH
"GOT HIS EARS ON"
"GREEN STAMPS"
STOP TOLL
"GREEN STAMP HIGHWAY"
"DEAD PEDAL"
"HAVIN' A CUPPA 30 WEIGHT"
CAFE
"SMOKEY"
Rosy's ROADSIDE MASSAGE PARLOR
CB SLANG
Advertising: a police car with lights turned on
Back door: the road behind or the last vehicle
Beat the bushes: lead vehicle looks for Smokey by going fast enough to draw him out of hiding
Bubble trouble: a tire problem
Eighteen wheeler: semitractor trailer
Front door: the road ahead or the front vehicle
Mobile parking lot: an automobile carrier truck
Plain wrapper: unmarked police car
Tijuana taxi: marked police car
Wall to wall: full scale reading on S-meter
CERTIFIED BUCKET MOUTH
BONAFIDE RATCHET JAW
"PICTURE TAKER"
SMILE! YOU'RE ON RADAR
"MALFUNCTION JUNCTION"
"THERMOS BOTTLE"
"BRUSH YOUR TEETH AND COMB YOUR HAIR"
"BEAR CAVE"
STATE POLICE
PRECINCT 8
I CANT
"CHECKING THE SEATCOVERS"
"10-4"
"PUTTING THE HAMMER DOWN"
"BEAVER"
I WILL
"10-100"
NATE OWENS
western graphics corporation

Traditionally, county and local police are believed to work to a quota. The revenue they gather from erring truckers and other motorists serves to bolster local funds. Both parties have been involved in this game since the beginning of road transport, but there has developed a degree of mutual respect. Each side recognizes the other as professionals, and this is amply demonstrated when things get rough out on the highway. If there is a wreck or breakdown, rockfall or other hazard, a cop will not be in the least surprised to find a trucker directing operations until the emergency services arrive. In serious emergencies, they both understand that they should be the last to panic. Being true pros, cops and truckers both share one vital factor; road sense.

The advent of Citizens' Band radio has added a new dimension to the game. In the days of the fuel crisis, CB became the trucker's means of organization, as well as his means of relieving boredom. CB has been around since the late Fifties, but was only used in a small minority of road vehicles. That was before the fuel panic – and the 55mph speed limit. The lower limit was intended to economize on fuel,

but truckers knew that this would not be the case for them. When a loaded rig approaches an upgrade, the driver must down shift, and this means running slower at a faster engine speed. It is obvious that he would want to approach the hill at the fastest possible speed. If he is forced to go slow, he will have to shift down sooner, using more fuel for less miles travelled. Some trucks are geared even higher, and the top ratio is hardly usable at 55mph.

Government and state authorities were unimpressed by the argument, but the truckers believe they were right and continued to press for a higher truck limit. They organized via CB and began to seek protection in numbers, travelling in convoys. A 'front door' and 'back door' take responsibility for spotting the bears, and with the assistance of other road-users along the way, they plot a fast, cop-free route. Police reaction is mixed. No doubt some officers resent radio, which they regard as their own weapon, being used by all. Official statements suggest, though, that as long as speeds come down, the police are satisfied. There is little doubt that CB encourages legal driving when there is a Smokey in the bushes.

Truckers are now in touch with each other (below and right) and with the rest of the world they pass through. In addition to Smokey reports, the drivers have plenty to talk about. They also have a language to say it in.

The Independent Truckers' Association aims to bring together those drivers who wish to improve their conditions (opposite). By running in convoy (left), they can keep in touch and beat the bears.

The cops have many new toys to keep the action spirited. These include various radar devices, some of which can give an instant digital reading of vehicle speeds in three lanes simultaneously, in any direction. Against that sort of technology, the road-user would appear to be at a distinct disadvantage, but devices are available which can detect these traps in good time. With names like Fuzzbuster and Bearfinder, these black boxes seem to set out to enrage the officers. Indeed, several states have made them illegal, although the careful trucker can hide one well enough to escape a casual inspection of his cab.

The policeman's lot is not made any happier by the ordinary motorist's enthusiastic adoption of CB. More and more private drivers have found that by listening in on truckers' conversations, they too can dodge the bears without difficulty. In March 1975, the price of a CB licence was cut from $20 to a mere $4, and this led to a rush. The numbers of new applications doubled every month, and by the end of the following year, more than six million permits had been issued. The demand was so great that temporary permits had to be introduced, to cope with the backlog that was building.

America is still the only country to have embraced CB on this scale. While CB has both good and bad implications, it must be recognized as the biggest single factor in the change of the life and working conditions of the long-haul man. Now the loneliness of the long distance driver is a thing of the past. Truckers are today in touch with each other, and the rest of the world through which they had previously only driven. Now they can answer back, speaking both as individuals, and with a common voice.

This is a major step forward, for the independent trucker has never been organized. The Brotherhood of Teamsters has made many overtures; some drivers do belong, but it is still unusual for the independent owner-operator to be a Teamster. However, the independents began to move toward a united front at the time of the 1973 oil embargo. They found much more to agree on than the simple issue of the speed limits for trucks. They also questioned the reasons for increased fuel prices, when the oil companies were making such vast profits. The last straw came when word got around the trucking community that supertankers were lining up outside harbors on both coasts, just waiting for the prices to rise.

The truckers, smarting from a feeling of helplessness and lack of representation in Washington, organized a shutdown. Feeling ran high and, in Ohio and Pennsylvania, there were confrontations with the National Guard. The more militant drivers went so far as to throw rocks and fire shots at other truckers suspected of being scabs. Many of these unfortunates were merely trying to make it home, and had no intention of stopping to pick up a strike-busting load.

The shutdown was not successful in raising the speed limit, or lowering fuel prices, but it did much to boost the Independent Trucker's Association. The ITA was the brainchild of Mike Parkhurst, editor of the truckers magazine *Overdrive*, whose offices were used as the communications center during the stoppage, and whose declared aim is the betterment of the trucker's lot.

The little guy now had a big voice.

Gear-Jammers

And their Good Buddies

The people who work the roads are as varied, and sometimes as colorful, as the country they drive across. Take Wild Billy and Wagon Wheel, for example. These two boys from Arkansas could not be more different and yet they make up a highly successful double team. Being from the same state, the two men speak the same language, and share a taste for country music, but there the similarities end. Billy, who is 25-years-old, is what might be called a bullshitter of the first degree, and an egotistical son of a bitch, in addition to being a bucket-mouthed ratchet jaw on the CB. He can be a dangerous person to be around, but he is, undeniably, a character.

The Wagon Wheel can give his partner a few years, and has a far more mellow outlook on life, partly due to the fact that he is married with three kids. He drove company trucks for years, mainly for a local carrier, and had achieved some seniority on the despatcher's board before he decided to walk out. Now he is happy to have a good driving job, although he always lets an owner know that he will not turn round and head back until he has taken his two days rest. The two men travel in a mighty Kenworth Conventional, powered by a 425hp Caterpiller, one of the most respected engines on the road. It is a high torque motor, which runs through a high-geared, 13-speed transmission, making the hills just disappear beneath the wheels almost as soon as they come over the horizon. They put 43,000 miles on the clock in the first three months of operation. The reefer trailer is packed full of frozen chickens in Arkansas, bound for California and Arizona. It returns with farm produce, which is run over to Mississippi. The two men try to log one round trip every

Wild Billy gets on to the CB radio as he heads onto the boulevard (left). His performance over the microphone is as flamboyant as his driving.

81

week with just two days off at home.

They admit that they do not quite know why they do it, but Wagon Wheel says that his daddy was a trucker, and that driving has now become an obsession. His father was involved in a bad wreck and, although he was unhurt, he never again wanted to see a truck. Soon after this, both his sons were trucking. Wagon Wheel has been a CB man since 1968. In those days, he ran a base station as well as a mobile. However, in the intervening years, he has lost interest in the radio as entertainment and now only uses it on the boulevard. He has met three other truckers with the same CB handle, and on each occasion was able to show them his first CB licence, which pre-dated theirs. In the face of such authority, the pretenders backed down and changed their handles. He can even remember the first time he heard the Smokey Bear handle. It was being used by a County Mounty in Rainville, Arkansas, back in 1969 or 1970 and was probably one of the first uses of that now familar name.

When Wild Billy gets onto that radio, he puts on a big show, particularly if his intake of pharmaceuticals has sent him into his own overdrive. With such a fast

rig, overhauling other 18-wheelers all day and night, his ego is continually boosted. While he is blowing the doors off the other traffic, he responds to their envy with a high-speed monologue, interspersed with tuneless harmonica-playing, or the almost endless repetition of Wagon Wheel's jokes. Most people find him entertaining, but many of the more solid, respectable types are probably glad to see him fly by and out of range, perhaps expecting to find this madman in a ditch somewhere down the road.

Billy did once wind up in a ditch. He was hauling swinging beef in a company truck, when a front wheel collapsed somewhere in Texas. He was quite badly hurt, although no one else was involved. People who know him say that he has become even wilder since then. Wagon Wheel is a steady driver; not for him the tire-burning antics of his partner. Hell, he can make as good time going at 80 or 85 as Billy can achieve at over 100. He respects the engine too. He figures that, apart from tire damage, that $4\frac{1}{4}$ Kitty Kat might well chew up the 13 Roadranger cogs and spit them out all over the highway if someone does not ease up on the hammer every once in a while.

Wagon Wheel takes the driving seat on his way home to Arkansas (below). The two partners (right) are seen in good humour alongside the big Kenworth.

Colonel Eagle, from Southern Georgia, has had many jobs driving for regulated carriers. The last one was good, paying 26 cents a mile. However, in the spring of 1977, the company decided to change to running double. This meant a co-driver and, although they could clock more miles, the 26 cents would have to be shared between them. This apparent cut in wages was too much for the Colonel and he went in search of further gainful employment.

He now runs for a private carrier, hauling plastic cups and buckets with an International Transtar tractor, supplied by a leasing company. Like many truckers, he spends a lot of time playing with his CB and Fuzzbuster. He runs a linear amplifier on his transceiver, which puts out such a strong signal that if you were to put a 100 watt bulb next to the antenna wire, it would light up. A 12 volt bulb would blow in just a few seconds – and that wire is insulated. He rarely uses the full 200 watts, but sometimes he will jack it up to listen in 100 miles up the road. In addition to Smokey reports, he listens for the oft-repeated jokes about Roadway drivers, the Polacks of the highway. His favorite is the one about the Big R driver who tried to beat a train over a railroad crossing. The poor guy hit the 42nd car.

Bill and Linda Myers sip their coffee in a 76 Truck Stop, somewhere outside St Louis, and wait for the girl to bring the baby food they ordered. Beside them, in a high chair, sits their two-year-old son Richard. As soon as the kid was old enough to go anywhere, he was traveling with Bill and Linda. Bill was always pleased to have his wife along, and he is delighted with the additional family passenger.

Wife and son not only keep him company, but Linda can handle the wheel while he relaxes on the double mattress. At first, he was terrified of her attempts to wrestle with the big Pete, but after a few days she picked it up. However, sometimes she still has to wake him up to help with a particularly awkward shift. Bill is pushing 50, and has been driving for five years since he left the navy. They have two other children, aged 14 and 15,

who look after themselves, or stay with friends, while mom and pop are away.

Linda does not go on every trip, and usually nothing will keep her away for more than a week. The family has been on a three-week trip, delivering machinery from the Detroit factories to all corners of the continent. Bill and Linda find trucking a rewarding and interesting business, particularly when they can take their time about the runs they make. They plan to slow it down over the next few years, and ease themselves into retirement gear. Bill hopes this will keep him trucking until the end of his working days, when his son may take over.

Colonel Eagle finds time to goof around before he hits the road (left). What else could this guy (above) be but a trucker?

Bob runs his Transtar 11 under the company colors of a heavy equipment hauler from the midwest. He is a country boy, who lives with his family on the edge of a small town in Wisconsin. Since he has been away on his latest trip, his wife has brought him a brand new motorcycle – a 400 Kawasaki, which they can both ride during his forthcoming weekend at home. Bob uses the CB handle 'Going Broke', and has to answer many people who want to know why he has not yet made it. Everyone they know, it seems has been going broke for years. Bob replies that he is a sight more stubborn than most, although he is the first to claim that most truckers are fools if they hope to make any money hauling exempt commodities.

Hauling for this regulated carrier, he picks up a good rate, and does not have to cut his prices, which he thinks would happen if the whole business was deregulated. He is one owner-operator who believes in regulation and big fleets. As long as these carriers continue to lease from owner-operators, Bob thinks the truckers have a good deal. He also thinks that the cost of fuel is in danger of forcing up prices – and people out of work – and is adamant that this too should be regulated. 'If the Government cannot bring it down, they should at least control it,' says Going Broke, belying his name as he heads up the bear-infested highways of his home state.

Cheryl Houston weighs in at 105 pounds, and measures only 4ft 11ins. She lives in Hollywood, California, and wants to be rich and famous. Since she claims to be America's Smallest Trucker, maybe she has already achieved the latter desire. She and her partner, Brandy Young, run an operation called Ladytruckers, which specializes in hauling rock group equipment for some of the bigger Stateside tours. They have already worked for Olivia Newton John, The Chambers Brothers, John Denver and Thin Lizzy.

They lease their trucks from major hire companies like Hertz, because the demands of the rock and roll business are so unpredictable. They have had as many as seven straight trucks and five semis

The Quazar Man (right) runs a White Freightliner out of his home town Los Angeles. He is seen here laying over in West Virginia with time to tidy up his tractor (below).

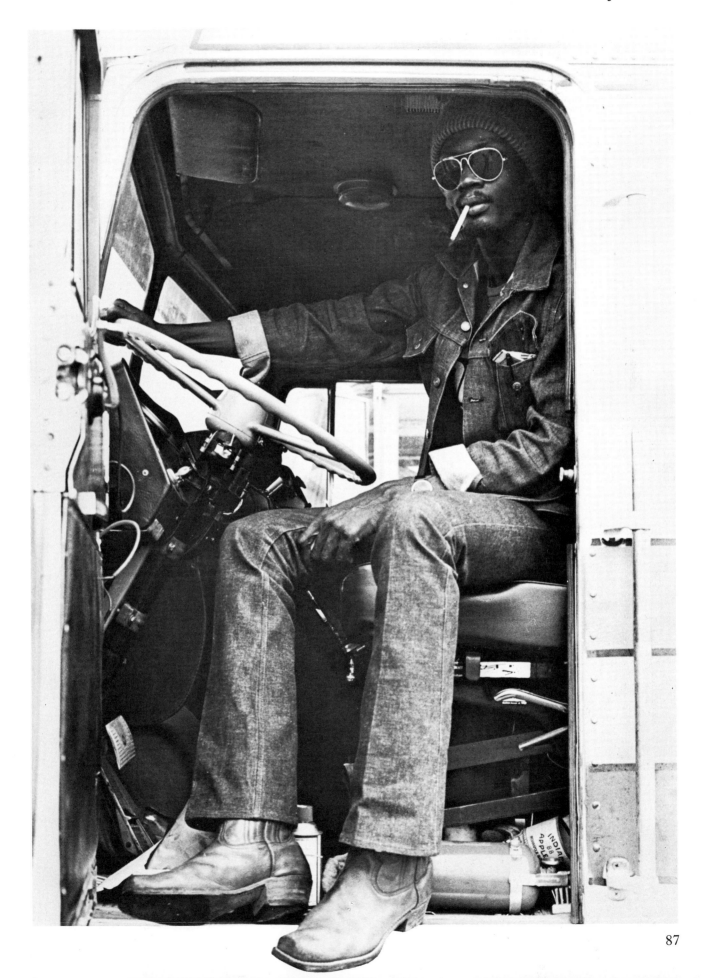

out on tour at one time. When that kind of workload comes up, they must obviously take on other drivers. Although they use some other women with California Class 1 chauffeurs' licences, they do occasionally have to employ men. This can make life tough for the long-haired male roadies, for they get upset about the name of the company for which they drive – and the effect it has on the other gentlemen of the road. They have often got into fights with macho truckers, who have a tendency to cast doubts on their virility and masculinity. Cheryl and Brandy came to their aid by using the name Fast 'n Easy as a cover for the men they sent into hostile territory. In some areas of the midwest, the girls claim that they too have come in for some rough treatment. They say they

LOS ANGELES (213) 656-1040

Ladytruckers (left) are in the music business. Alan Baxter (below) is in the produce game. His KW and reefer outfit cost him $80,000 and is seen here on its first run to LA. The silver paint job is non-standard and the pin-striping cost on top of that. Even the wheel nuts are chromed. The double-sleeper rig is fitted with a 425hp Caterpillar and a 5X4 duplex transmission for running over the mountains from his Nebraska home to the West Coast.

89

Truckers need friends in many places. Mr Birdsong (above) handles Peterbilt parts, and the badge-covered waitress (right) probably earned her trophies pouring hot coffee.

inevitably, wonder why such a girl as Cheryl does it. The answer is simple: she likes to feel master of such a big machine.

The Brush hangs around the Alameda Street Truck Terminal, in downtown Los Angeles. With his battered van, his palette and brushes, he is well-known to the drivers. He has been painting signs on trucks for more than 13 years, mostly putting a quick name on a door, or sometimes a big 'Keep On Trucking' design on the front of a trailer. Most of the names he paints are CB handles, and The Brush is proud that his artwork is seen all over the country. Truckers from such far-apart places as Ohio, Carolina and Oregon have carried Brushwork past millions of Americans. It is probable that this man's work has been seen by more people than have ever been inside an art gallery.

After so many years around the truckers, The Brush thinks he knows them pretty well. He has an idea that most of the guys share an identical dream: 'To be going down the road with a good paying load, and a rig that suits his style – one that makes him feel good – with his name painted on the side. He picks up a beautiful beaver somewhere down the road, and that makes him feel even better, and makes all the other drivers feel real jealous, and she rides with him forever. That's what most truckers dream of.'

A pump jockey at Alameda Street disagrees, and observes that most truckers are fools. He should know, he says, for he was driving himself for 15 years. 'That truck cost me my wife,' he says. 'It's a lonely job. You never know anybody, or have any time to see any place. You just have to hang around these truck shops with all the hustlers and the pedlars. See these guys here? They've all got something to peddle, maybe pills, or jewelry, or else they're pimping. They know the truck drivers are fools, they'll buy anything, either to keep themselves happy, or else to take home to their wives. When they get home, they find that their woman's run off with some guy.'

They come from all walks of life and all parts of the country. In the East and Midwest, the number of Interstate jobs keeps many of the city boys close to home, but out West, or in the rural South, a

have been raped just once too often!

Ladytruckers have the same problems as most women drivers when they pull up at a truck stop. However, most of the women truckers are somewhat larger and more easily recognized than these two girls. Often, waitresses simply refuse to believe that they are entitled to sit at the 'truckers only' section, and refuse to serve them. The threats of a semi-trailer coming through the window usually makes the doubters see reason.

Ladytruckers claim to be only the second legal rock and roll trucking company in the country, being in possession of I.C.C. and P.U.C. authority to haul anywhere, in or out of California. People,

trucker can really run. The drivers from those parts do not like running too far East or North into Yankee country, and a lot of the Yankees prefer not to head into the deep South or too far West. The Westerners complain about the Eastern turnpikes, where they cannot cut loose. On the New York Thruway, there are toll booths every 15 miles. 'Those people nickel-and-dime you too much,' is the complaint. For the Easterners, the South Western states can seem too wild: too many truck stop commandoes, too much emphasis on the gingerbread and fast trucks, too many guns and crazy cowboys.

The fact remains that most Interstate truckers have at least seen most of the country and they know where they feel comfortable, for most of them get no further than the roadside wherever they are, and that appears to suit them fine.

It's not hard to tell the Eastern drivers from the Westerners, although the rigs often give a better indication than the personal style. The Maryland Ford (opposite) does carry some extra cab marker lights, but is otherwise very basic. The two drivers on this page show obvious preference for western dress.

Truck'em up Stops

Looking for that 100-mile smile

With coast-to-coast and border-to-border runs keeping truckers away from home for weeks at a stretch, the United States is demanding more of its long haul drivers than ever, and certainly more than most other countries in the world. To make life a little easier, a complete range of vital services has grown up at the roadside. As the big rigs continue to roll day and night, drivers and operators can be assured that if the schedule is threatened by any unforseen circumstance, they will find all the assistance they need close at hand, within the confines of their enclosed world. In the past, when the roads were still only two lanes wide, and the traffic was so much lighter, fuel and food stations could be found at crossroads, or at the edge of town. Customers parked at the roadside or, if mechanical help was needed, there may have been a place at the rear for a mechanic to look under the hood.

The stops that became really popular, either because of good food, cheap fuel or convivial atmosphere, were easy to spot: they were the ones with a long, long line of trucks pulled up on the shoulder. As the traffic began to outgrow the highways, parking lots were added. The four-wheel travelers really began to home in on the noted oases, but the great days of these establishments were already numbered. Nostalgically referred to as Mom and Pop stops, they could always be relied on to provide a warm welcome for the long haul driver, and an opportunity for him to jaw with his road buddies. Waitresses would soon get to know the men, and the warmth of their smiles would see them just about as far down the road as a cup of the 100-mile coffee that the girls dispensed – and would be just as

The line of trucks pulled over at the side of this Ohio state highway (left) in the 1950s, indicates a popular stop for truckers on the night run.

95

good a reason for the driver to return as the quality of the food.

The development of the Interstate system virtually wrote an end to that era, for it brought the massive, all-providing truck stop, thriving on the long haul traffic. They may offer super-efficiency, but gone is the personal touch. These days, a driver may see a few familiar faces, but if he is on a 2,000-mile run, particularly out in the wilds of south or west, it is no longer likely that he can arrange to meet up with a friend traveling the other way.

The new oil company-owned complexes, the Truck Plazas, Havens and Terminals, which regularly punctuate the interstate system, are the modern equivalent of the old-time staging post, supplying the driver's back-up, and providing facilities for the maintenance and service of his vehicle. The most common reason for a trucker to roll into one of these stops is, of course, to take on fuel. The larger establishments are able to fuel as many as 20 tractor trailer outfits

Drivers hanging out close to the roadside at a 1950s stop (right), while a pump jockey (below) attends to a gas truck.

at one time. The really big outlets sell upwards of 20,000 gallons a day. With truck tank capacities of up to 200 gallons, refuelling takes some time and the usual procedure is for the driver to leave his rig in the hands of the pump jockey while he heads inside to refuel himself.

Pump jockeys themselves usually have more than a passing interest in trucks. Often, they are youngsters with their own dreams of becoming long haul drivers; occasionally they are older men who have given up the road, but cannot make a complete break from the trucking scene. As the pumps dispense the number one or number two diesel, the jockeys snap into a well-rehearsed routine. The windshield, mirrors and lights are cleaned off, including the rear and turn lights;

water, oil and fluid levels are checked, and the tires bumped to check for flats or slow punctures. If the driver requests it, the inside of his cab may be cleaned out, ashtrays emptied, and the inside of the windshield cleaned. At some places, where turnover is rapid, the jockeys will even move the trucks away from the pumps to make room for new customers. However, at most stops, drivers have plenty of time to finish off a snack while the rig is occupied at the pump island.

Regular lubrication of an over the road vehicle is absolutely essential to its well-being and survival. When a truck is a long way from home at service time, independent or fleet operators will often choose to have a lube job done at a convenient truck stop on the route. Parts needing

Union 76 Auto/Truck Stops are one of the largest and most ubiquitous of the oil company complexes. Pump jockeys (below) check on fluid levels, while the driver attends to his log book.

The larger stops offer truck wash facilities (right), but for many drivers a cup of good hundred-mile coffee is reason enough to use a truck 'em up stop (above).

adjustment or replacing should also be attended to as quickly as possible, so any large truck stop owner will find his garage and maintenance facilities in almost constant use. Agents for various engine manufacturers may also be based at strategic truck stops, along with repair teams to work on refrigeration units.

The Tuscon Truck Terminal – or Triple T – in Arizona, is one large truck stop ideally placed to cater for reefer operators. It is located on Interstate 10, some 60 miles from the Mexican border crossing at Nogales, and most produce haulers pass by on their way east. Temperature control is vital if the fruit and

vegetables are to survive their journey, so refrigeration engineers are on call 24 hours a day. Another facility in regular use, particularly by the owner-operators, is the truck wash. Operated by Truckomat, these large-scale versions of the regular car wash can be found at many of the stops. While not cheap – the price for washing a tractor alone may be $15 – the service is popular with drivers who want to keep their vehicles looking smart. In some cases, a wash is free with every 100 gallons of fuel. At smaller locations, attendants will climb all over the truck with brushes and hosepipes, doing the job in the traditional way.

Whatever services a truck 'em up stop may offer, there is still no accounting for taste. You can lead a trucker to a stop, but you cannot make him pull in, if he prefers a rival establishment just along the road. Even such a well-established stop as the Triple T does not have anything like a monopoly in its immediate area. About one mile east, on the same side of the Interstate, is located a Texaco stop. Although it does not offer as many facilities, it usually seems to have as many rigs pulled up in the lot.

Several truck stops are often sited within a few miles of each other, each offering different services and fuel. Apart from mechanical resources, the stop must cater for the trucker himself. Many places have a Western Union wire service, bunk house or lounge, restaurant, post office, or even a wider range of clothing, gifts and accessories than its neighbourhood rivals.

There are two basic types of truck stop: those offering a full service and those

Giant signs entice truckers from miles around. Marie's (opposite) has been by-passed by Interstate 10, the Commercial (above) is in downtown Los Angeles, and the Mid Continent (left) is right on the highway.

supplying fuel or food. It is not uncommon for rural gas stations, sporting a diesel pump or two, to announce themselves as truck stops. County and state highways are still dotted with diners or cafes catering for local delivery drivers. The Pepsi or Dr Pepper sign outside often describes the establishment as a Truck Stop. The smaller fuel stops are particularly attractive to the owner-operator. By providing self-service pumps, it is often possible to cut the price of the fuel and make it a real bargain for the man with a thirsty 450hp rig. With the large quantities of fuel needed, every cent, or even tenth of a cent, is important. Some places calling themselves truck stops do not even sell fuel, but cater more for the physical comforts of the drivers. A certain stop in West Memphis, Arkansas, hands out business cards for a pill pedlar, who rejoices in the name Peashooter.

Female companionship is something that most truckers have to do without most of the time, but that does not stop them thinking about it, and spending a lot of time searching for it. When the lonely driver has worn out his fantasies, and gazed at a few magazine center folds, he may decide the time is ripe to visit some such establishment as Rosie's Massage Parlor, or the Lucky Lady Lounge. More likely, the frustrated fellow will settle down at the rear of some big truck plaza and spend the night calling into his CB for a willing female. There are, of course, many women ready to cater for the needs of truckers, just as there have been in coastal ports, or western cow towns. A few hours with a CB radio in the vicinity of a truck stop gives a real insight into the lives of truckers and the operations of the pavement princesses – and those other women who reach out from their beds through the airwaves to tease and provoke horny truck drivers.

It is possible to hear Lady Dynamite, a well-organized madame, checking up on one of her flock, asking where she is and whether she has finished. The Sweet Thing, of which there are many, tells

The Triple T (preceding page) is one of the larger independent stops, offering full facilities. Kelly's (right) is also a full service stop, but the Blue Bird is only a garage. Truckers even have their own cafes, this one (right) is in downtown LA.

Some truckers have to resort to Go-Go girls for their entertainment (below). Others keep the family together by traveling together, like this couple with child (opposite).

Lady Dynamite which part of the lot she is working. She has been there for a couple of hours, talking with the men in their tractors, while the madame has been down the road at the next truck stop, seeing to the affairs of her other ladies. By the time her 'recreation vehicle' arrives at the rear of the next parking lot, Sweet Thing and her tricks are heading towards her through the shadows. Of course, many drivers do not wish to leave the comfort and familiarity of their sleepers, and they can be serviced as an out-call. Lady Dynamite, however, would rather be in direct control of all situations.

The T-Town Fox does not get too

close to the truckers, partly because of her boy friend, and partly because of her own excellent sense of self-preservation. She prefers to remain a CB voice, while lying at home on her water bed, supposedly practising all manner of do-it-yourself variations, described in detail for the benefit of her male listeners. She claims to be too young to leave the house, and too innocent to get mixed up with the big and brutal truckers.

Much of the jawing that goes on over the CB is crude, but most is harmless. While it gives all kinds of freaks the opportunity of getting under the skins of righteous citizens, it also offers a way of easing those long hours or days spent waiting at the terminal for return loads.

Sunset truck stop (opposite) is situated outside Tucson, a town with many facilities for truckers. Other stops (left) attract custom with magazine advertisements.

Down at Nogales, for example, there must be hundreds of trucks at any given time. On some busy days, there will even be thousands. Many of these independents will have been there for a day or two, waiting for a load.

Down there, Channel 19 is continually buzzing with requests for rides home, jokes, arguments and all other ordinary and strange conversations of a community of laid-up wanderers. One man needs to get home to Texas. Asked if he can drive, he replies that he would not be much use, because he has just wrecked his truck and his legs have been burned so badly he can hardly walk. His wife has just had a baby and he wants to get home to see her. After a few repeats, he goes off the air, presumably having been rescued by a fellow Texan.

A female trucker, with the handle Squeeze Easy, gets into an argument with a bucket mouth who is obviously drunk, and offensive with it. A young voice keeps on asking for the time, and the drunk responds in a negative and insulting manner. Squeeze Easy's com-

panion, the Beaver Squeezer, suggests that the drunk washes out his mouth with Jack Daniels. This produces a few laughs and leads to a conversation about getting loaded. 'What kind of loaded you be looking to get?' a voice asks. 'You be looking for some pharmaceuticals, or some of that whacky tobaccy?' 'Oh, no, you rascal,' comes the reply. 'We be talking about getting the trailer loaded, get us out of this crazy place, don't cha know.'

Truck stops all over the country have their own atmosphere, in addition to reflecting the attitudes of the particular region in which they are located. Many try to offer a service that truckers will not be able to resist returning for. The Mom and Pops generally stand a better chance of keeping their regular clients, although they will almost certainly not be able to draw many away from the oil company-owned complexes.

A typical independent truck stop is Al's, just off 1–30 outside Hot Springs, Arkansas. Before the Interstate was built, Al had a useful location right out

At Al's truck stop (preceding page), truck washing is still done by hand. Down in Nogales, one trucker looks delighted to have company (below). Other trucks stand empty while the drivers are in town.

on the old US Highway. When he was bypassed, he moved his whole business a few miles to stay close to the super slab, and his livelihood, and opened up a few hundred yards north of where a small highway intersects the Interstate. In the traditional style of many smaller stops, the restaurant and fuel facilities are owned by different people, and they occupy separate buildings at each side of the lot. Al's is a regular fuel stop for several out of state carriers, including a Texas-based company, responsible for moving oil products to the midwest.

With so many interstate trucking companies located in the southern and western states, it is not surprising that truck stop operators from the north and east travel many miles to negotiate exclusive fuelling and service agreements for the various fleets. The majority of truck

Truck stops are for truckers as the sign (right) clearly states. Of the rigs lined up below, several are from south of the border.

stops are independently owned, and most of the better ones are members of the National Association of Truck Stop Operators, NATSO, whose members all offer complete facilities for the trucks and their drivers. From a fleet operator's point of view, it is often worth paying the slightly higher fuel costs at the big stops, in return for the knowledge that if repair or wrecking services are ever needed, the prices will be controlled. The independent one-truck operator, running through such a place as Odessa, Texas, might be well-advised if he fuelled up at a cheap self-service place like the Red X, a small establishment, where the restaurant service is cheerful and, more to the point, the diesel is cents cheaper than at the next stop further down the road.

Whatever a truck stop can do for a vehicle, it is often the human qualities that bring drivers back every time they are in the area. A stop like the Mass 10, just off the Massachusetts Turnpike, has so many things going against it that the drawbacks are even featured in the advertising used to attract customers. Mass 10 is well-known to truckers as The Dump. However, until they have actually been there, people do not realize what a dump it really is. In the words of the establishment itself, 'it aint convenient or easy to find'. What it does offer is a very personal service, with an owner who lives on the premises, a free bunkhouse, and even a lake where off-duty truckers can fish or swim away the summer afternoons. It also accepts just about every known credit card.

There has been much criticism of the way in which the large operators have handled the take-over of smaller chains. When Union 76 took over the Pure truck stop chain, they added the word 'Auto' to the Truck Stop sign. Many customers have since come to resent what they see as preferential treatment of tourists, who are allowed to park their cars closer to the restaurant, and sometimes seem to get faster service. However, the standard of shower and wash facilities is as high as it should be at any truck stop. A clean stop is a good stop.

There must be as many ways of gaining, or losing, custom as there are roads across the nation. Now that the old-style

Americana has been replaced almost everywhere with concrete and plastic oases, one truck stop looks pretty much like another. Things such as companionship, straight and pleasant service and a relaxed atmosphere are, therefore, most important if return visits are to be considered. Little events like the photo competition run by the Abilene Truck Stop, or such glossy temptations as the casino at Nevada's Boomtown are the things that keep the truckers rolling back.

This stop (left) could only be in Texas. It is, in fact, the Abilene Truck Stop which runs a photographic competition in conjunction with a trucker's magazine.

The wreckers

Rolling them back up is the duty of specialist wreckers and their crews. Although many truck-stops and garages can despatch a wrecker, they often travel hundreds of miles to a wreck. Whether clearing a blocked highway or simply lifting a truck on to a trailer, the wreckers are kept pretty busy. They can be smartly turned out, too.

The Media

Information or truxploitation?

The midnight-to-dawn radio shows do a great deal more than keep their trucking audiences informed and entertained; they keep them awake – and alive. Indeed, until CB really took off as a means of two-way communication, those disc jockeys across the country, and the odd amphetamine, did more than anything to keep road-weary eyes fixed on the black top ahead of them.

If there was a truckers' top 10 of disc jockeys, it is certain that Charlie Douglas of WWL, *Way Down Yonder in New Orleans*, would occupy a favorite position. WWL is a clear channel A.M. station, broadcasting on 870, and it can be heard across most of the Southern states. The Douglas show is built around the inevitable country music, with particular emphasis on trucking records. It also includes personal messages to the drivers, and much vital information about weather and road conditions and many of the commercials are aimed specifically at the trucker.

The rival KWKM station from nearby Shreveport, Louisiana, takes the trucking bias one stage further with its Night Rider Show. It is actually broadcast from a remote studio at Kelly's Truck Terminal, and presided over by Big John Trimble, who brings his listeners a similar mixture of country sounds and trucking information. This show must be the only one broadcast live from the roadside, although segments have been recorded in truck cabs by other dj's.

Other stations attracting a regular trucking audience, include WWOK, covering the Florida region, WBT of Charlotte, North Carolina, whose d-j Larry James claims to be heard from Maine to Miami, and WWVA, from the appropriately named Wheeling, West

Virginia. WLW, of Cincinnati, Ohio, claims to reach from Canada to the Keys, and in Iowa there are two stations serving truckers: WHO, of Des Moines, and KXWL, out of Waterloo. Further west, the midnight-to-sixers can pick up the Denver station KERE, hosted by the popular Tim Larsen, while Seattle's KAYO broadcasts Trucker's Club 1150, presented by Dan Williams. On the same side of the Rockies, KLAC's Phantom 570 show from Los Angeles features Chuck Sullivan.

Even the most modestly-equipped truck will carry some kind of sound system, such as a tape player, but there really is no substitute for the personal communication and close relationship existing between the trucker, struggling

PHANTOM 570
KLAC TRUCKERS CLUB

All over the country, truckers
are kept informed by the many
special shows, which invariably
run from midnight to dawn and
help to keep them awake.

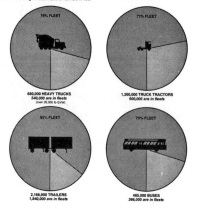

Fleets, the biggest operators of commercial vehicles

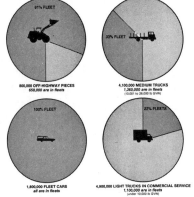

Commercial Car Journal has been around for some time. Although aimed at buyers of new vehicles and fleet operators, it contains articles of interest to drivers.

to keep awake and alert, and the man talking to him over the airwaves.

The service performed by the stations is more important than most people realise. Requests and messages can be relayed by CB to the stations and phone calls from truckers' wives are often relayed to the men at the wheel.

The commercials are sometimes minor classics. General Motors ran a series of trucking songs with funky arrangements and hard-driving lyrics that waited until the very last line before making the first mention of the GMC Astro, the product they were aiming to sell. Transtar Rose, otherwise known as country singer Bonnie Nelson, gives out road reports, and lets truckers know where they can meet her and be brought fully up to date on the latest news from International, the makers of the Transtar range. Other commercials sell everything from oil filters to job opportunities.

When the trucker finally decides to pull off the highway and switch off his radio, he will probably find the time to bury his nose in his favorite magazine. Even here he is not far away from business, for the magazine will in all probability be one of the trucking publications some of which have been around for almost as long as the big-wheelers themselves. *Commercial Vehicle* and *Commercial Car Journal* were around as far back as 1911, primarily as market guides for fleet operators.

However, truckers did not really have a magazine to call their own until *Overdrive* first appeared in 1961. This publication is undoubtedly the most outspoken of the bunch and could even be one of the most up front magazines of any kind. It sells at $2.50 ('The Price Of Truth') and claims to be The Voice of The American Trucker. Politics and legislation are dealt with seriously and at great length. Crusading editorial policies often bring it into contact with Senators, Congressmen, and even the White House. *Overdrive*'s single-minded concern is to carry the banner on behalf of the independent trucker, no matter how complex or explosive the issue in question. There have been frequent clashes with the Brotherhood of Teamsters over fraud and corruption exposés.

The Price of Truth **$1**

OVERDRIVE

NOVEMBER 1972   *THE VOICE OF THE AMERICAN TRUCKER*

These matters, and analysis and criticism of new vehicles, occupy the heavyweight pages of the magazine, while the lighter side offers the traditional and welcome diet of pin-ups. Of course, these days many truckers are women, and *Overdrive* has always taken a positive and enlightened stance on the issue of equal facilities and acceptance of the ladies behind the wheel.

The color pages usually feature a monthly gallery of some of the fanciest rigs, under the title of Tractor of The Month, in addition to Dump Truck of The Month, and even Wrecker of The Month. The back of the magazine includes such excellent circulation-boosters as cash value coupons which entitle the holders to cut-price or free services at truck shops. If the reader redeems every coupon, he will have more than covered the cost of the magazine.

Owner Operator, a bi-monthly publication, retails at half the price of *Overdrive*, but its less frequent appearances means that it cannot cover the same amount of ground. As part of a large publishing group, it does not have the same trailblazing spirit, and much of the material is of a more general nature. The magazine proclaims its dedication to 'the success of the independent trucker', and its readers presumably prefer its less flamboyant style and its matter of fact

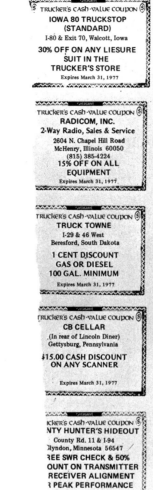

Overdrive was launched in 1961 as the first real 'truckers' magazine. The covers and truck pin-ups (left) attract the drivers, while coupons (above) give added value.

Brady Reed of Carrollton, Ohio, has logged over 400,000 miles on his "Iron Butterfly" since he purchased it in 1973, but it still looks as good as the day that he took delivery of this blue and white beauty. The power train below the body of this wide-front Transtar 4300 consists of a NTC-350 Cummins engine, Fuller RTO-9513 transmission and Rockwell 4.11 ratio 38,000-pound rears.

The IH tractor is made to look like the work horse that it is by the addition of the third Snyder fuel tank. Altogether, the tractor can carry 240 gallons of diesel. Chromed and polished items sparkle from every spot on the International, including the Alcoa aluminum wheels, the fuel tanks, the entire exhaust system and the bumper.

The International tractor rides on 10 x 20" General steel radial tires and the 1965 Ravens 38-foot trailer sits on 10 x 20" Dunlop rubber on Webb wheels. The Ravens has three axles — each spaced nine feet apart — and is capable of carrying a legal 75,000-pound payload in Michigan and Canada. The front trailer axle is a cab-controlled air-lift axle which makes it easier to negotiate tight turns without scrubbing off tire rubber. When the trailer is not loaded to capacity, the air-lift axle is carried off the ground.

Brady Reed leases his services to Detroit-Pittsburgh Motor Freight of Cleveland, Ohio, and hauls steel products with his 200-inch wheelbase IH in Ohio, Michigan, New York, Indiana, Illinois and West Virginia.

Melvin Strickland, of Mt. Airy, North Carolina, is the proud owner of this 1976 Kenworth and 1976 Utility trailer. The bumper, fuel tanks and Alcoa front wheels are all polished aluminum. All the other wheels are chromed steel.

The KW's cab and sleeper are padded in gold naugahyde upholstery. The cab interior also sports a padded steering wheel, an air-ride driver's seat, an AM/FM/8-track tape player, a 23-channel CB radio, and a Fuzzbuster. The many gauges are set in a simulated woodgrain finish dash. The cab floor is covered with a blue shag carpet.

The cab-over covers a 350 Cummins engine which throws the power to a 15-speed Fuller transmission and the 4.33 rears. The 1976 Utility trailer is a 45-foot lightweight, designed with stainless steel front, back and side doors. It is cooled by a Thermo King unit with polished aluminum doors.

Bill Smith of Mt. Airy is the trucker who logs the miles in the driver's seat of this KW for Melvin Strickland, hauling refrigerated products throughout the Southeast.

reporting. The two rivals are not generally on sale at the same outlets.

Open Road is a much thinner publication than the Big Two, and it costs only $1. It is published at Fort Worth, Texas, and has a definite folksy feel, although a wide distribution prevents it from becoming too parochial. *Open Road* is, in fact, less about the road than the men who travel on it, for the majority of the articles are chatty pieces about the truckers and their families, or nostalgic glances at the great old-timers who are still going strong. Although the magazine appears to be aimed at the older age group, it does sponsor all-night radio shows all over the country.

Another, more recent, publication at Fort Worth, is *Eighteen Wheeler*, which describes itself as the official publication of the National Truck Drivers' Hall of Fame. It produces 24 pages of a lighter-than-usual mixture of happy snaps of truckers, letters and fiction. There are no editorial photographs of trucks at all, and the advertising is primarily bought by Texas companies. The Hall of Fame, headed by 'internationally-known artist and muralist' Joe H. Williams, calls itself a non-profit organization, dedicated as 'a shrine to honor the nation's truckers for their skill, safety and heroism, courtesy, co-operation in crime prevention, and citizenship'.

Truck Tracks is definitely provincial, if the preponderance of Oregon-based advertisers is anything to go by. It has been on the market since 1968 and is produced on a lower budget than the others. However, it does manage to feature some interesting articles, and maintains a good relationship with most of the truckers who pass through the state.

Truckers have much to be thankful for in the area of magazines, and so does the accessories industry, which could hardly maintain the same high level of trade without advertising on radio and in the press. Decals are central to most sub-cultures, either as proclamations of loyalty to certain brands or activities, or merely to raise a smile. At the same time, they make a gesture of independence in a monotonous world.

Just after the Second World War, the

Through the 1960s and 70s many truckers' publications have come and gone. Of the survivors, Owner Operator and Open Road have an established readership. Eighteen-Wheeler (opposite) is a new publication.

FOR THE DRIVER BEHIND THE WHEEL

35¢

18 WHEELER

Copyright © 1976, Jack Reed and Friends, Inc.

Vol. 2   NATIONWIDE DISTRIBUTION   No. 2

The official publication for THE NATIONAL TRUCK DRIVERS HALL OF FAME

WHAT KIND OF CITIZEN ARE YOU...
LAW BREAKING
or Law Abiding?
Are The Highways Safe For Other Drivers When You Are On The Road?

Not if you're to believe the words to most of the so-called "truckers" songs. Don't think for one minute the general public isn't drinking in the words to these songs and forming the opinion that YOU are the world's worst and most inconsiderate driver.

It doesn't matter if you've driven five million miles without a scratch, if you've stopped and assisted every driver you've ever seen in trouble, YOU are being condemned. In their minds, YOU are the driver who will run a trooper off the road, YOU are the driver who will form a "convoy" and disregard every traffic law and safety regulation in the book. (Can you imagine using the same singer who recorded the song, "Convoy" to make recordings on driving safety? It's being done!)

You can change this image you're being stuck with.

In putting this magazine together, we drive many miles every month. We've yet to find the first inconsiderate trucker. We've seen, and heard on C.B., many cases of truckers stopping to give assistance when other drivers were speeding right on past. We know that you couldn't stay on the road hour after hour, day after day, if you were the type driver described in the songs.

We also believe that most drivers do not hear those so-called truckers songs except when played on the juke box at one of your stops. Just how much time do you spend listening to the radio stations playing that type music and how much time do you spend on C.B. radio?

Are you willing to prove that you are a sensible, law-abiding driver?

The 18 WHEELER has been in contact with several states' highway department leaders. They agree that you are the finest and safest drivers in the world. They would like the public to realize this.

Continued on page 15

WHO WOULD DUMP THIS?
We got this picture of DIANE at an exhibit of dump trailers at a recent convention She's just one of the many reasons for holding a convention in Houston.

NATIONAL TRUCK DRIVERS HALL OF FAME
pages 6,12,13

'M JUST RUCKIN' AROUND

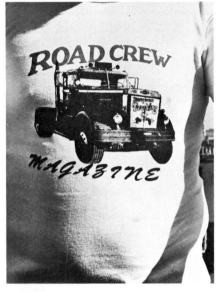

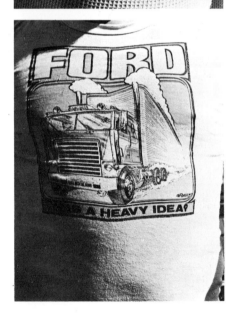

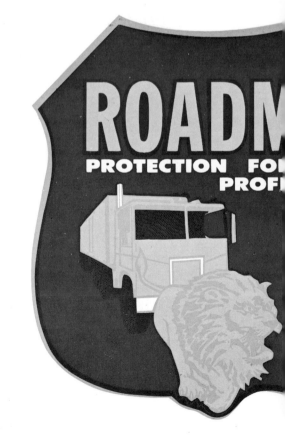

T shirts and decals proclaim status as well as raising a smile. The word 'truck' is especially handy for slogans because of it's rhyming association.

Mack caravan toured the country, carrying with it a back-up supply of advertising novelties such as cigarette lighters, ashtrays, neckties, and even golfballs. Soon after this, they brought out diecast model trucks. This, however, was merely the first trickle of what has in the succeeding years become a flood. Almost every manufacturer offers various promotional gimmicks. Zippo lighters, and the many imitations, complete with famous truck

KEEP ON TRUCKIN

TRUCK IT!

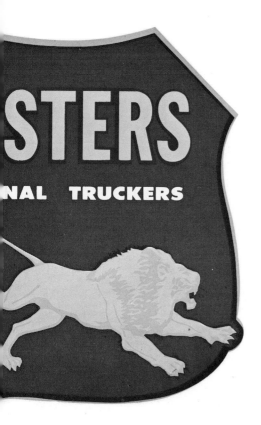

STERS

NAL TRUCKERS

OVERDRIVE TRUCK INFORMATION RADIO

CROSS COUNTRY CB'ers

I'D RATHER BE TRUCKIN'

badges silk-screened on the side, are available at truck stops. There are also belt buckles in enamel or rough cast, and the inevitable T-shirts of all shapes, sizes and designs.

Children's T-shirts are emblazoned with the message 'My Daddy's A Trucker' and, in these liberated times, 'My Mummy's A Trucker'. If the homebound trucker has any loose change left in his pocket after shelling out for his fuel, he will find a series of scale models of trucks,

A trucker can add to his wardrobe from the counters at many truck-stop shops. Goods sold include everything from caps to boots.

1/25 Scale Trucks

AMT's line of massive over-the-road trucks and trailers is the most extensive in the hobby kit field. They're authentically scaled from the manufacturers' official blueprints.

T529 Chevrolet Titan 90 Cabover

T510 GMC Astro 95 Cabover

T535 Mack R-Series Conventional

T560 "Movin' On" Kenworth Conventional

T526 Autocar A64B Conventional

T519 Kenworth W-925 Conventional

T502 Peterbilt 352 "Pacemaker" Cabover

T501 Peterbi "California H Conventiona

T520 Kenwor K-123 Cabov

T530 White-Freightliner Single Drive Cabover

T537 Diamond Reo Conventional

T818 Caterpillar D8H Bulldozer

T533 Peterbilt Wrecker

some containing up to 250 parts in the tractor alone. Board games such as 'That's Truckin', or 'Convoy', are also big sellers, particularly at Christmas.

If the trucker really feels like spending, he can buy himself a pair of Wrangler Trucker boots. Identical in style to the cowboy boots beloved of most drivers, these leather items feature an embossed design of a conventional tractor, with a big 10–4 in place of the traditional western-type scrolls.

Somewhat less damaging to the wallet are rain cheaters and caps, carrying truck stop names, or makers' logos. These are the independent's answer to the uniforms worn by the fleet drivers. Other items to add status to the trucker's wardrobe are cloth badges of CB clubs, drivers' associations, or elite groups such as roadeo winners and Roadmasters.

More than 30 years on, Mack is again a big name in the novelty gift market, with a range of blanket rolls, floppy hats, women's blouses and even baby boots, all manufactured in red and blue bulldog check. They also offer antique-style model table lamps, chrome ashtrays, and even a stuffed Brockway 'Huskie'.

Models and toys (opposite) may be for kids, but these half-size P.I.E. Peterbilt models are working outfits used for promotion purposes.

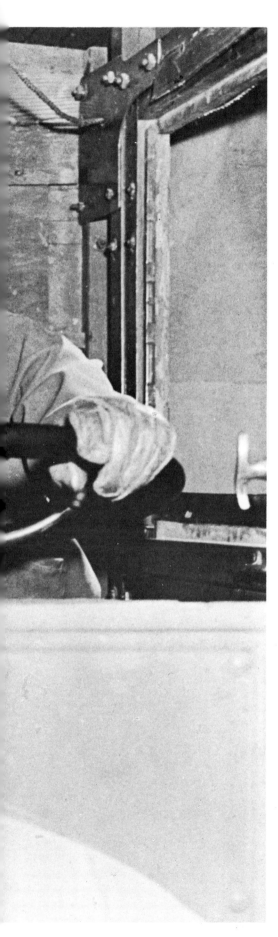

Wheels on Reels

Motion Pictures from the highways

The trucking scene offers action and adventure on a wide-screen scale, with freedom stretching away for mile after mile of open highway. However, disappointingly few of these vivid and evocative images have been sought, let alone captured, by the movie camera.

The handful of movies featuring the world of the big rigs has been more concerned with trucking as a mere backcloth, against which a standard Hollywood story is played out. Instead of trying to create realistic over-the-road dramas, filmmakers have grabbed the soft option of re-hashing the clapped-out plot in which the little guy struggles for survival against a vast ruthless organization determined to wipe him out in every sense of the word.

The good-against-evil conflict of the screen has moved into the 20th century, with the traditional Western hero having to do what he had to do, being overtaken by cops and robbers, who are now in turn being hard pressed by the urban vigilante and the occult anti-hero. However, whether on hooves or wheels, the pursuit of riches remains the most common screen activity. The independent trucker would seem to fit the modern version of the stereotype hero, who has dashed across the screen from the earliest days of movies. He can be pictured as the individual, a man standing alone in the best traditions of the American dream, as seen through the Hollywood view-finder. His mission, like that of the Pony Express rider, or the Wagon Train master of a century before, is simply to deliver the goods. The only difference is that the horsepower has multiplied and the trail has turned into a modern superhighway.

However, the movie industry has failed to recognize the obvious parallels,

Bogart, Ann Sheridan and George Raft head down the road in 'They Drive By Night'. The two brothers are partners in a one-truck outfit.

and the usual trucking plot pushes our hero nearer to Kojak than Gary Cooper. Rarely does the movie trucker have to face the real problems of life on the road: bad weather, long hours, brake failures, dangerous loads, or hallucinations. Determination is the real fever in the blood which drives the trucker on in his fight to make a decent living.

Driving sequences were featured at the start of *They Drive By Night*, the first, and some say best, trucking film ever made. Directed by Raoul Walsh in 1940, the movie starred Humphrey Bogart, George Raft and Ida Lupino. Bogart and Raft played two brothers running a single truck on the West Coast. Corruption lurked around every bend in the road, and while struggling to keep their business alive, they drove when they should have been sleeping. The inevitable crash cost Bogart his arm, after which a place was found for him in the garage, while his brother went on to take over a fleet of the latest trucks, not to mention the previous owner's wife.

The early shots of the pair as they trucked through the night on wooden seats, rain hammering through the canvas side-flaps, and feeble headlights picking out the muddy road, conveyed at least some idea of the conditions. The coffee shops and the eye-prickling weariness of the all-night run, were all there.

It was not until 1955 that the next

On location, shooting a scene with George Raft maneuvering the Kenworth truck (top). The two brothers before the wreck (below left). Raft survives in one piece (center) and goes on to become a major fleet operator.

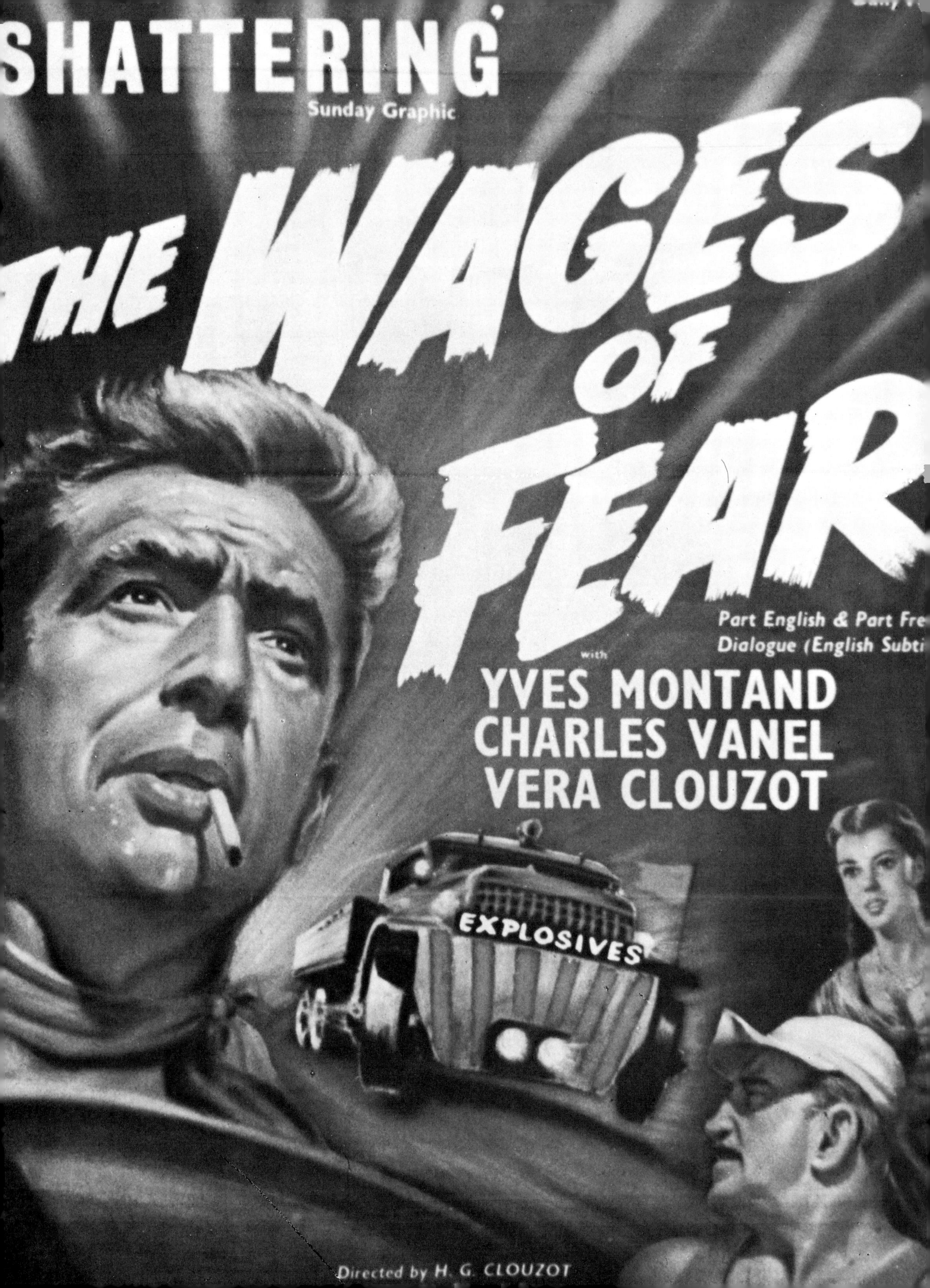
SHATTERING
Sunday Graphic
THE WAGES OF FEAR
Part English & Part Fre
Dialogue (English Subti
with
YVES MONTAND
CHARLES VANEL
VERA CLOUZOT
EXPLOSIVES
Directed by H. G. CLOUZOT

trucking film appeared. An interesting French production shot in South America, it made the 15-year wait worthwhile. The film was called *Wages of Fear*, and starred Yves Montand as the driver of a nitro truck making a hazardous journey over rough tracks and weak wooden bridges, which collapsed beneath his wheels. This was authentic adventure, full of suspense to the end. It remains one of the finest and most exciting trucking films ever made, as well as one of the very few which was able to extract the essence of the job.

Hollywood and Detroit sprang to life almost at the same time and primitive cars featured in the earliest movies. Since then, the auto has become an integral part of most contemporary films, almost matching the importance of the actors. Stunt-driving is a growth industry and the tricks have been pulled so often that there are textbook methods of staging them.

Audiences are so accustomed to motorized disaster, that they expect a car to go over a cliff, or explode in flames, more often than it has a flat tire. While the public readily accepts the star quality of an automobile, and appreciates its speed, racy lines and obvious sexual impli-

cations, the first film actually to star a truck, took most people completely by surprise. Unfortunately, it also offended a high proportion of truckers. The reason was that the truck, an anonymous five-axle, tanker semi-trailer, was the black villain of the piece, an evil creature which the average car-owning cinemagoer had no hope of understanding.

Duel was made for television in the late 1960s, although it was subsequently shown in theaters. Truckers complained that it showed them in a bad light, although the actual driver in the film was never seen. Set in the natural location of the South West desert, the story concerned a homeward-bound salesman and his nightmare confrontation with the big, dirty, awesome monster. His attempts to overtake the truck were all

'Wages of Fear' (left) a 1954 French movie starred Yves Montand and Charles Vanel along with an ex-army truck loaded with nitro. The action was shot in South America.

thwarted. The rig replied with a selection of the most brutal tricks in the roadhog's repertoire.

The car-driver did manage to pass, but his red compact, and his nervous driving, were no match for the tanker, and the duel of the title commenced. The truck driver was hidden behind a tinted windshield and, until the end, there was no hero – just the car and its driver, the truck and some roadside spectators. The motorist eventually found a way to fight back and, in a spectacular surprise ending, he became the hero figure, suitably framed by a movie sunset.

Another made-for-television film of fairly recent vintage was *Hijack*. This was a mainstream trucking plot, concerning a load for a Government agency, attempted robbery, off-road sequences and average ironic ending: there was no valuable load at all, they were simply acting as decoys.

Movin' On, the television series that ran for two seasons, certainly had its faults, but it was better than the usual nothing. It might even have opened up some network minds to the possibility of another, more solid, trucking weekly. It is a tragedy that television has to be so ratings-conscious, because programs always seem to lose out to the lowest common denominator. *Movin' On* was not too far removed from *Peyton Place*. It may have rolled on wheels, but it was pure, soft, mild soap opera.

Although the rig was the star of the show, Kenworth, who hired it to the film company, obviously did not want it battered or scratched doing silly stunts. Consequently, Will and Sonny, the show's two heroes, were rarely seen 'on rubber' and spent so much time sorting out other people's problems that they hardly had time for any driving at all. When they were seen in the cab, there was little of the atmosphere found in a genuine rolling home. Certainly, they would wish to keep their $60,000 investment nice and clean, but they must have spent more time in the truckwash than on the highway.

The title sequence, with Merle Haggard theme song, and split screen images of polished big wheels rolling over the concrete, always promised much more than this show was ever able to deliver.

Kenworth's expensive prop appeared in most of the outdoor shots, usually occupying the middle distance, just to remind the viewers of what they were watching – and possibly sell a few more for KW. Maybe the makers of *Movin' On* should have spent a little more time watching re-runs of an earlier trucking cult series of the 1950s *Cannonball*.

Dennis Weaver (above) the human star of Duel about to be terrorized by the big dirty Pete. The truck smashes up a snake farm (far left) before going over the top.

'Truck Stop Women' (above) featured more trucks than naked women, but was only an R-rated feature. In 'White Line Fever' (right) the hero takes up the gun to protect his wife and livelihood. (Overleaf) he bobtails down the road, chased by the local Smokey.

Another aspect of the trucker's lifestyle became the subject of two exploitation movies. In 1972 *Night Call Nurses* featured a truck driver, several energetic ladies and a little revolutionary adventure. Two years later, *Truck Stop Women* was released. It was directed by Mark Lester and concerned the exploits of a team of females who run a truck stop as a front for a prostitution and hijack racket. Movie buffs will not be at all surprised to learn that this operation attracted the interest of the mob. The girls played the old roadside breakdown routine out in the desert. The first trucker to stick his head under the hood was promptly relieved of consciousness, and his truck. The characters actually seemed real enough to pass as road people. Director Lester showed that a big feature budget is not necessary to inject the feel of road dust into a film. Indeed, the biggest slice of money must have been spent on the stunt-driving sequences, which were excellent.

Truck Stop Women was not just a soft core skin flick, but it did provide one sequence which rates as the purest piece of trucking cinema. Accompanied by Red Simpson's *I'm A Truck*, the narrative took five as we witnessed a superb, fast cut series of rolling rig shots from all angles; from bridges looking down, and roadsides looking up, from every lane, against dawn or sunset, in desert, on freeway, in the mountains. This visual treat worked better and said more about the potential of these great 18-wheelers than all the feeble trucking plots put together. Clearly, a truck freak was involved somewhere in the making.

White Line Fever, directed in 1975 by Jonathan Kaplan, involved a bit more travelling, but not many more trucks. The hero was a solo independent trucker, just back from the Vietnam war. He came up against the ubiquitous mob (surprise) in his unflagging efforts to earn enough to keep up the payments. The brokers would not give him work unless he carried contraband. He was an upstanding fellow and refused. He decided to go

it alone, but had to carry a gun to protect himself and his wife. Together with some like-minded fellow truckers, he fought the corruption that spread from big business chiefs, to dock workers, and even the local State Trooper.

The hero's big Ford cabover, Blue Mule, was the target for homicidal motoring mobsters, and at one point he had to pull off an incredible stunt to keep them at bay. Taking over the shotgun from his vigilante co-driver, he clambered onto the trailer roof and rolled along until he hung over the side of the truck and blasted the enemy clean off the road. Unfortunately, there were few touches of realism, such as the time when the hero was woken from a doze at the wheel by another trucker coming up behind and calling him on the CB. However, the thrilling stunt sequences made up for this lack.

The finale was exciting enough to raise the movie above the average run of trucking spectaculars. The stunt was set up by Carey Loftin, who staged the auto

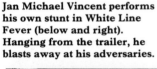

Jan Michael Vincent performs his own stunt in White Line Fever (below and right). Hanging from the trailer, he blasts away at his adversaries.

scenes for such movies as *Bullitt* and *Vanishing Point*. He took the Blue Mule up a ramp at 70mph and crashed the $30,000 truck through a glass sign that cost the studio three times as much to build. This alone was enough to raise the movie to the status of big rig spectacular.

Vanishing Point and *Two Lane Blacktop* were both shot entirely on location, either in or around a fast car on a cross-country run. They demonstrated quite clearly that the involvement of drivers with their vehicles, and the compulsion to lay rubber from coast to coast are ingredients which could generate a great movie about the trucking experience. However, it might need a talented trucker to communicate the feeling of running on big wheels. Unfortunately, there seem to be few budding film directors on the great highways, so we shall simply have to wait for the definitive truck movie.

Truckers have been featured in many films, usually as a means of getting the

guy out of the house for longer than the usual nine-to-five haul. There have certainly been some eccentric attempts to portray the figure. Burt Lancaster's performance in *The Rose Tattoo* leaned heavily on the stereotype horny trucker. In *That Midnight Kiss*, things got completely out of hand with a chubby Mario Lanza bellowing forth in the unlikely guise of a singing trucker.

The 1962 film *Lonely Are The Brave*, featured Kirk Douglas as a cowboy living out of his time. The final, ironic blow that kills his horse, and possibly him too, was delivered by a truck carrying a load of privvies. No man can stand in the way of progress. The truck's impending arrival was noted throughout the movie, and the message made clear: it is the modern trucker, and not the cowboy, who now travels the length of country unimpeded by fences.

Trucking Toons

The rhythm when he's rolling

The romance of the road, like all good romances, has always had an appropriate musical backing – a chunky beat, with a bluegrass swing or shuffle, leaning heavily on electric bass and rhythm guitars.

Although the big rigs have undoubtedly taken over the glamor of the railroad, along with the business, they have yet to inspire a commercial classic to match those hymns to the great steam loco. Railroads and trains such as the Wabash Cannonball, Atchison Topeka and Santa Fe, Orange Blossom Special, and the Rock Island Line, are already indelibly written into the musical history books, together with disasters such as The Wreck of The Old 97.

The first trucking disc appeared in 1936, a not-very-memorable ditty called *Trucker's Ball*. Three years later Decca released two versions of *Truck Driver's Blues*, written by Ted Daffan and sung by Cliff Bruner and Moon Mullican. The trucking song had made its tentative debut, but hundreds more were to come and go before the first national hit in 1963 – Dave Dudley's *Six Days On The Road*.

Throughout the Fifties and Sixties, countless country artists produced records reflecting the massive movement from railroad to highway, the nation's new vital supply line. Most of these songs are now, deservedly, forgotten, and many of the performers have long since moved back into more traditional country music.

The overall quality of the lyrics does not reveal many literary pretentions, usually punching out some simple and fairly obvious piece of homespun morality. The vocal track is almost always mixed right up to give prominence to the telling of the story, which is ren-

In tune with the trucker . . . the Willis Brothers came up with the first version of an apt road-song (right) which still gets re-releases.

dered in a typical relaxed growl.

The Starday label, founded in Houston, Texas, in 1952, by Harold W. 'Pappy' Daily, specialized in a brand of rough-hewn honky-tonk country music usually heard only around the Texas-Louisiana border. This style was responsible for some of the best trucking sounds on record, with the electric guitars complemented by pedal steel and fiddle combinations. This lent itself superbly to the feel of compulsive movement and heart-bending sentiment attached to the lonely guy out there on the road.

While the teenage audience drove around listening to the more commercial rockabilly sounds, Starday punched out hundreds of singles, many of which were trucking specialities. Some were destined to become minor standards, but others, long since gone, were produced in such small numbers that even specialist dealers have trouble in tracking them down.

Lonnie Irving's distinctive electric bluegrass sound carried some of his numbers to moderate success, but others, like *Pinball Machine*, *Gooseball Brown*, and *Trucker's Vitus*, were to become favorites. Johnny Bond was another early Starday artist, and he achieved some success with *Hot Rod Lincoln*, a four-wheeler song which was re-released in 1975. The Willis Brothers came up with the first version of the hit song *Give Me Forty Acres* (to turn this rig around), which has since been re-released several times, and is still able to produce a chuckle from the least musical of truckers.

Starday kept things moving with *Long Haul Weekend*, *Diesel Smoke on Danger Road*, *Truck Stop Cutie*, and more. Frankie Miller appeared with *Truck Driving Buddy*, while Hylo Brown was the man responsible for the first, and probably best, version of Terry Fell's *Truck Driving Man*.

Lyrics were not always considered essential, and some offerings contented themselves with attempting to communicate the feel of moving down the road. Consequently, many instrumentals were given appropriate titles, among them *Trucker's Ramble*, and *Gear Shiftin'*, by Tommy Hill, who had a head start working as a recording engineer for Starday.

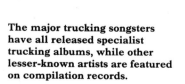

The major trucking songsters have all released specialist trucking albums, while other lesser-known artists are featured on compilation records.

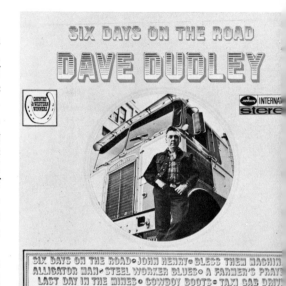

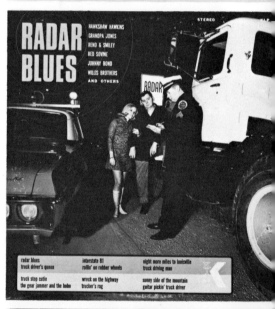

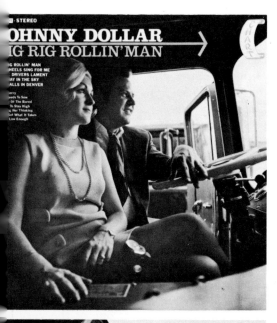

The Big-Rig Sound

Lots of trucking tunes were produced by small labels, particularly in the Texas-Louisiana belt, during the Fifties. They are often difficult to find today, but here are some typical titles:

There Ain't No Easy Run	Dave Dudley
I Can See You In The Windshield	
Chick Inspector	Dick Curless
15 Gears, 14 Wheels	
Bulldog Mack	Mike Hoyer
Our Sleeper Cab Home	Pat and Darrell
Gears, Ridge Route	Johnny Bond
Widow Maker	Jimmy Martin
Hot Wheels	Stan Farlow
Convoy In The Sky	Willis Bros
Curves And Inbetweens	Ray King
Big Wheel	
10 Days Out, Two Days In	Joe Maphis
Riding Down Ole 99	
Kiss And The Keys	Red Sovine
Movin' On	Merle Haggard
Girl On The Billboard	Del Reeves
Backing to Birmingham	Lester Flatt
Interstate 81	Don Reno and Red Smiley
Rolling On Rubber Wheels	Stanley Bros
Radar Blues	Coleman Wilson
Road Stop	Jimmy Day
Big Rig Rollin' Man	Johnny Dollar

More up-to-date, and certainly more obvious to the prospective collector are the following titles:

Truck Stop Cutie	Willis Bros
Trucker's Paradise	Del Reeves
Truck Drivin' Cat	Jim Nesbitt
Truck Driver's Wife	Joyce Ferdon
Truck Driver's Nightmare	Larry Scott
Trucker and The UFO	Brush Arbor
Blue Truck Driver	Jim Ashford
How Fast Them Trucks Can Go	Claude Gray
Truck Stop Salvation	Jimmy Buffett
Truck Driver's Sad Story	Chuck Hubbel
I'm A Trucker	Johnny Russell
Truck Driver And The Hippies	Red Simpson
Truck Driver's Queen	Jimmy Martin
I Believe He's Gonna Drive That Truck To Glory	Craig Donaldson

The King Label, which merged with Starday in the Sixties, also had a catalog of trucking records, including some western swing-style numbers by Charlie Moore and Bill Napier, who scored modest hits with *Lonesome Truck Driver*, *Truck Driver's Queen*, and *Guitar Pickin' Truck Driver*. Jimmy Logsdon was another King performer, with a slightly obscure piece called *Gear Jammer*.

Red Sovine was, without doubt, one of the most consistant sellers on the truck music market. In the Fifties he had hits with the talking-style *Giddyup and Go*, and later with *Phantom 309*, the spooky tale of Big Joe, a ghostly trucker who came back from the dead to give lifts to hitch-hikers. This is, incidentally, one of the few references in trucking songs to this mode of travel.

Freightliner Fever, one of his more recent singles, discusses the taking of pep pills, referred to as uppers, speed, bennies, whites or blacks. He sings, 'It's a big black pill, so long and round. To a driver, it's the West Coast turnaround'.

Dave Dudley, a former baseball pitcher from Wisconsin, is one of the most popular trucking song stars. Although many of his songs suffer from arrangements that are too basic, they are still among the finest that the trucking genre has yet produced. His Mercury albums include such fine songs as *Wreck of The Old Slow Binder*, *Jacknife*, *Speed Traps Weigh Stations and Detour Signs*, *I Got Lost*, and *Two Six Packs Away*. A later album, *Keep on Truckin'*, is a disappointment for the fans. The title song has a brassy, pop arrangement, and Dudley's present day situation is well summed up by the title of another song on the album, *I Fly Everywhere*.

Red Simpson's album *I'm A Truck* is highly recommended as one of the very best collections of trucking tunes. The title number has been a big juke box hit, and was also featured in the movie *Truck Stop Women*. This West Coast album is more sophisticated than most of its trucking contemporaries. While some of the tracks are ballads, a few roll along at a

Cowboy hats are as much a part of the truck driver's wardrobe as of the country stars. The Willis Brothers (facing page) recorded for Starday, the same label that featured mini-skirted girls (right) on their albums by 'various artists'.

STARDAY RECORDS

GRAND OLE OPRY

THE WILLIS BROTHERS

Atlas Artist Bureau, Inc.
110 TWO MILE PIKE-GOODLETTSVILLE, TENN.
(615) 859-1343

155

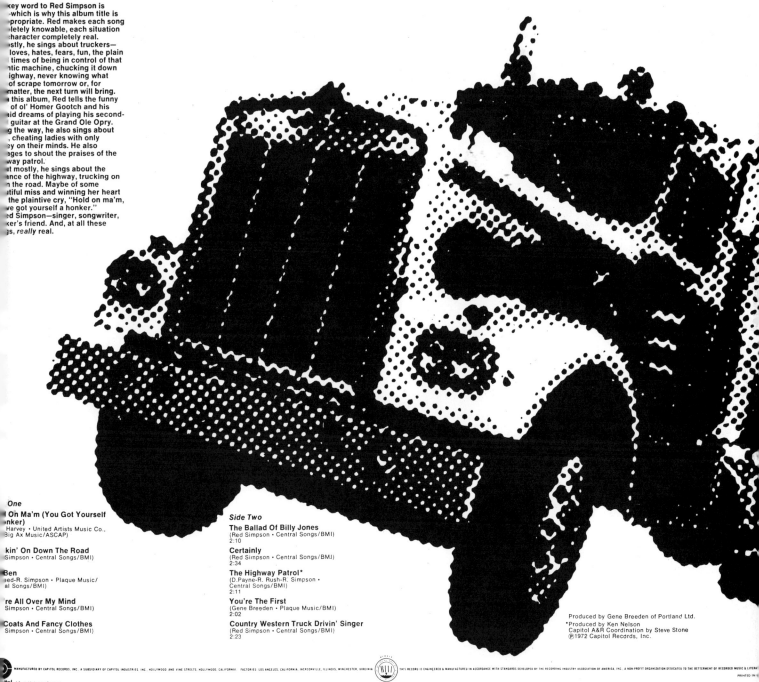

THE VERY REAL RED SIMPSON

key word to Red Simpson is
—which is why this album title is
appropriate. Red makes each song
pletely knowable, each situation
character completely real.
stly, he sings about truckers—
loves, hates, fears, fun, the plain
times of being in control of that
ntic machine, chucking it down
highway, never knowing what
of scrape tomorrow or, for
matter, the next turn will bring.
this album, Red tells the funny
aid dreams of playing his second-
guitar at the Grand Ole Opry.
g the way, he also sings about
, cheating ladies with only
ey on their minds. He also
ages to shout the praises of the
way patrol.
t mostly, he sings about the
nce of the highway, trucking on
the road. Maybe of some
tiful miss and winning her heart
the plaintive cry, "Hold on ma'm,
ve got yourself a honker."
d Simpson—singer, songwriter,
ker's friend. And, at all these
s, *really* real.

One

Oh Ma'm (You Got Yourself
nker)
Harvey • United Artists Music Co.,
Big Ax Music/ASCAP)

kin' On Down The Road
Simpson • Central Songs/BMI)

Ben
ed-R. Simpson • Plaque Music/
al Songs/BMI)

re All Over My Mind
Simpson • Central Songs/BMI)

Coats And Fancy Clothes
Simpson • Central Songs/BMI)

Side Two

The Ballad Of Billy Jones
(Red Simpson • Central Songs/BMI)
2:10

Certainly
(Red Simpson • Central Songs/BMI)
2:34

The Highway Patrol*
(D. Payne-R. Rush-R. Simpson •
Central Songs/BMI)
2:11

You're The First
(Gene Breeden • Plaque Music/BMI)
2:02

Country Western Truck Drivin' Singer
(Red Simpson • Central Songs/BMI)
2:23

Produced by Gene Breeden of Portland Ltd.
*Produced by Ken Nelson
Capitol A&R Coordination by Steve Stone
℗1972 Capitol Records, Inc.

most satisfying pace. His song, *Black Smoke Blowin' Over 18 Wheels*, ranks as one of his best, along with *Runaway Truck*, which he wrote with Buck Owens.

In 1965, Dick Curless hit the national country music charts with *Tombstone Every Mile*, a story of a ride through Hainesville Woods on 'a 41-mile ribbon of ice'. Written by Dan Faulkerson, the song eventually became the best-selling country song of the year. Curless never quite managed to repeat this success, although in 1970 he did well with *Big Wheel Cannonball*, a reworking of *Wabash Cannonball*.

One of the most perceptive trucking

Some of the singers of the classic truck driving songs. (Top left to right) C. W. McCall, Dick Curless, with (bottom, left to right) Dave Dudley, Lonnie Irving and Red Sovine. Above: the artwork on the back of a Red Simpson album.

157

Two more Starday albums which featured girls along with trucks on the sleeves.

songs must be the 1968 release *Looking at The World Through a Windshield*, sung by Del Reeves and written by Jerry Chestnut and Mike Hoyer. Although there is no evidence that either singer or songwriters have any trucking experience, some of the observations on this record, and the way they are put across, have a feeling of authenticity. These are the songs of the road, the corny old jack-knife tales, waitress tales, hamburger tales, runaway trucks, brakes failures, and other such emotional themes as the heartache of Man away from his Woman. In the finest traditions of country music, some sound like unadulterated mush . . . but, it is mush from the heart. Some slight feeling for country sounds is essential, or the listener will not get a thing out of it.

Country music has won a far wider audience over the last decade, and this

Del Reeves (above) is super-imposed alongside an old Jimmy while looking for a Truckers' Paradise on the United Artists album.

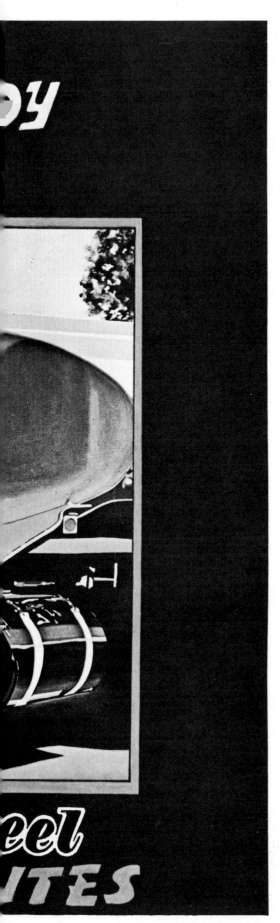

The Commander (above) is no longer supported by his Lost Planet Airmen, but their album (left) remains one of the best rock/country fusions. The California Pete on the cover was brushed by his brother Chris.

new enthusiasm has brought it right into the cities. Among the groups who helped this movement was Commander Cody and his Lost Planet Airmen. While they played mostly old rock and boogie tunes, their music was laced with country styles, and in 1972 they made an album on the Paramount label called *Hot Licks Cold Steel* and Truckers Favourites. The album cover featured a painting of a Peterbilt Conventional, and the artist was Cody's brother, Chris Frayne. The tracks fully lived up to the cover, with such titles as *Truck Stop Rock, Truck Drivin' Man*, and the amazing *Mama Hated Diesels*.

The Byrds were another West Coast group who came around to country music by way of Bob Dylan songs, and they featured Lowell George's *Truck Stop Girl* on their album, *Untitled*. The Flying Burrito Brothers also headed for the open highway and, in addition to coming up with a frenetic version of *Orange Blossom Special*, have made several versions of *Six Days on The Road*. However, one of the best recordings of this song — and certainly the furthest away from country — was the rhythm and blues arrangement recorded by Taj Mahal on his album *Giant Step*.

The big CB boom in 1974 was another boost for trucking tunes, and a top-selling record called *Convoy* by C. W. McCall brought the trucker's CB jargon into everyday usage. Two years later Red Sovine just about wrapped up the CB song craze with *Teddy Bear*, a sickly ditty about a crippled boy.

Heavy on the Gingerbread

Custom trucks and new ideas

The many options on 'standard' trucks, to make them roll faster, longer, safer, straighter and cheaper, are almost matched in the catalog by the many shiny, tempting chrome and polished aluminum fittings with which the proud new owner can beautify his rig. Fleet trucks may need nothing more than the basics, but the owner-operator is not likely to be so easily satisfied. He will undoubtedly wish to put some eye-catching shine on his vehicle, some hint to the world that an individual personality, rather than a drab corporate identity, is at work behind the wheel.

Aluminum comes a lot lighter than steel, so it has many practical advantages and is regularly used on fuel tanks. It can also be polished to a brilliant gleam. Chrome is commonly used on cab bullet lights, grab handles, and sometimes the bumper. If the rig is going to be seen anywhere at all, there will also be obligatory chrome smokestacks.

The shine really does attract those truckers, as evidenced by the selling pitches mounted by the various truck makers. Peterbilt sell their vehicles on their Class, and even the workhorses can be dressed. For example, International's

This Kenworth VIT (left) sports a fancy paint job that is definitely not from the factory. The Peterbilt (below) has been given a KW-type finish.

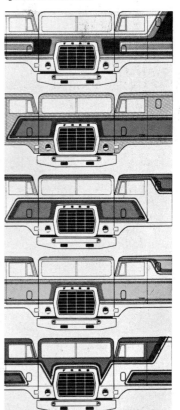

The Brush (far left) makes a decent living painting signs on owner operator's rigs. The White cabover (left) and the Ford paint schemes (below) are aimed at the independent market. Many leased trucks (below, left) carry individual paint treatments.

Transstar brochure eulogises its optional chrome bullet lights as adding that 'masculine' touch to the truck. Even Luberfiner, who make those cylindrical tank-shaped exterior filters sell hard on the glories of chrome. In one of their radio ads, they used a sweet-talking seductress of a country girl to woo prospective customers, and one of her major selling points was the chrome which, she implied, turned her on.

Trucks, such as Kenworth, Peterbilt, Freightliner Powerliner, and Mack Cruiseliner, which are aimed at the owner-operator, or the small fleet market, would never dream of appearing in an ad without full chrome; but neither would the lower priced workhorse trucks, like White, Ford and International. It is even stated that a custom-built truck with full chrome and comfort interior is competitive in price with a standard truck equipped with all the options.

However, when the trucker starts looking at the options on custom built rigs, he will very soon find himself in another, highly-expensive world. Interior kits include everything from air suspension, factory-installed CB radio, and separate air conditioning for the

sleeper, to insulation and carpets for the cab, which can also be upholstered in hyde. As with most aspects of the truck sales business, all it needs is cash.

Obviously, the ambitious truck stop commando will require a custom paint job. There are specialist truck spray shops only too willing to oblige, but very few will be able to come up with a fancier-looking scheme than the factory – so the trucker should think about his color-scheme right from the start. Even if the owner cannot afford to compete in a beauty contest with chrome smoke-stacks and suchlike, he can enliven even the drabbest of trucks by having his name, slogan or CB handle painted on

by hand. These little personal touches are not limited to owner-operators. Fleet drivers too may wish to lift their rig out of the uniformity of the bunch, and they are often quick to add their own mark.

If the wallet-busting array of chrome stacks, guards, air horns, handles and spotlights still do not make the rig look quite like the outfit the trucker has always dreamed about, he can always smother it with marker lights. Some semis driving by night look like rolling casinos, or a circus on wheels, with orange, red, white, blue and green flecks outlining their shape. The last two colors are not acceptable to the law, but that does not seem to diminish their popu-

Many truckers favor small grilles on their cabovers to allow room for the paint (left). Both KW (below) and Freightliner (bottom) are aimed primarily at the owner-operator.

The sun shining off this trailer (preceding page) shows off the stainless steel to good effect. Mexican rigs (above) are dressed in their own kind of style. These chrome goodies (right) are on sale at the Peterbilt dealers.

larity with the decor-conscious truckers. Down Mexico way, drivers favor illuminated Madonnas and religious paintings. There is, though, little to beat a mirror-polished smoothskin trailer, cruising through a sunny day.

Having fitted out the truck to suit his own personality, the trucker may wish to further demonstrate his masculinity by competing with his peers. In this, he is no different from auto drivers who have had the urge to race since the early days. The competitive trucker has the oppor-

tunity to show what he can do at various roadeos, jamborees and festivals, entering in all manner of driving tests and games; but only recently has he got into that particularly American pastime of drag racing.

Circuit racing is, of course, ruled out, but burning up a hot quarter mile is reasonably safe. While speeds may only range around 74mph in 17 seconds, few truckers can resist the temptation to take part. Spectators seem to be equally enthusiastic, for more than 10,000 turned

up at the Ontario Motor Speedway, California, for the first official meeting, in February 1976. Some 80 diesel tractors entered and did battle over the quarter mile course, with eliminators in eight classes, depending on horsepower and number of axles. The whole thing is a scaled-up version of pro drag racing, with size making up for the lower speeds. There are no rolling burnouts, but plenty of smoke shooting from those stacks, and the sound of the big Cummins and Cat diesels adding up to music in the drag fan's ears. Dump trucks, wreckers, and even a concrete mixture, took part in the early rounds. The meet was a big enough success for a Trucker's Grand National event to be staged only

four months later, at Kansas City, Missouri.

One of the highlights of the Ontario event was a demonstration run by Jerry Malone's Super Boss truck, and it achieved the fastest time of the day. This awesome rig was not eligible for the contest, for it could not be called an over the road tractor. The highly-modified '64 Kenworth sports a chrome-plated Detroit diesel 12V twin turbo-charged motor, which develops a full 1,000hp. Stripped of mirrors and horns, the cab has been lowered at the front and fitted with a high-mounted rear spoiler to keep the 10 × 20 rear slicks on the road. Malone can run the quarter in 13 secs, with a terminal speed of more than 90mph. He aims to boost this to 150.

Super Boss set Malone back $150,000. It is not his first expensive creation, and it probably owes its existence to a 40ft frozen whale. Showman Malone was exhibiting this cool colossus, and he needed a show vehicle to haul it around. The one he built was a KW known as Old Blue, and it was followed by the inspiringly grand-sounding Boss Truck of America. This is also a KW conventional and it featured double sleeper boxes, all the chrome imaginable, and a gold-plated fifth wheel. Not surprisingly, Malone does not drive the Super Boss to shows. For that he has yet another KW,

OVERDRIVE MAGAZINE

PRESENTS

SAT. JULY 17

BOSS TRUCK OF AMERICA

SUN. JULY 18

WORLD FAMOUS TYRONE MALONE

GRAND NATIONAL
TRUCKERS
DRAG RACE
CHAMPIONSHIPS
TRUCK RODEO

KANSAS CITY INTERNATIONAL RACEWAY
KANSAS CITY, MISSOURI

RODEO EVENTS SAT. JULY 17

FOR MORE INFORMATION CALL RODGER WARD 816-333-1556

DRAG RACE SUN. JULY 18

this time a Cabover, three-axle, straight job with a long, low specialist body – and, of course, its own big share of gleaming chrome and fancy paintwork.

Jerry Malone, never one to miss out on the main chance, or a spot of alliteration, changed his name in 1977 to Tyrone, the Daredevil Diesel Driver, in tune with his ambition to become the fastest trucker of them all. However, as a record breaker he was up against some stiff competition. At Bonneville Flats in 1975, two ordinary working truckers, Harold Miller and Larry Lange, piloted Liberty Belle, a modified 'stock' Kenworth to a diesel record of 132·154mph. Neither man had any previous experience of record-breaking, but they shattered the diesel best time set in 1971 by racer Bill Snyder. After working through nine gear shifts on the five-mile run to the Flying Mile, driver Miller had a further $1\frac{1}{2}$ miles in which to shut down.

However glamorous it is, all the speed and spangles are of secondary importance to the real function of the trucking business: the economical distribution of freight. Since the great fuel crisis everyone, from fleet king to independent, has been primarily concerned with reducing fuel consumption. Many people have been trying to conserve energy for many years, but the traumatic months which saw rising fuel costs and sinking speed limits sent a shock wave through the trucking world. Since then a whole new industry has sprung up, bringing the science of aerodynamics to trucking.

The basic problem in moving any object as large as a tractor trailer outfit is the size of the vehicle itself. Fuel and rubber are burned up at an alarming rate, and the transmission and engine strains to keep the thing moving on down the road. Half of this massive effort is used up in resisting aerodynamic drag as the high, flat-fronted vehicle pushes the air out of its path. There has been a big move towards air-deflection devices. Although effective on all box body vehicles, the deflectors are particularly helpful to cab-over tractors.

Research into the problem of drag on commercial vehicles began in 1953 at the University of Maryland, and was reviewed by N.A.S.A. in 1974. Several big freight haulers have been using them for many years, and recently many more have followed suit. Many of the devices now available look ridiculously simple, but they do deflect the airstream over and around the trailer. In 1975, GMC became the first motor manufacturer to produce their own deflector. It was built

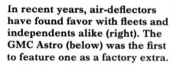

In recent years, air-deflectors have found favor with fleets and independents alike (right). The GMC Astro (below) was the first to feature one as a factory extra.

Big engines like this Cummins (above) can prove to be as economical as smaller ones. Tire-drag (right) is another factor for the economy-minded trucker to consider.

specifically for the Astro cabover and was a double curvature unit, mounted on the front of the cab roof, just behind the bullet lights. Results from wind tunnel tests showed a significant reduction in drag, and a corresponding saving on fuel. Called the Dragfoiler, it was road-tested on a Mayflower rig, which was fitted with other fuel-saving devices, and turned in even more impressive results.

Other streamlined afterthoughts which can be added to a semi, include rounded corner pieces for protruding motors in front of a reefer box, and spoilers running along the trailer top leading edge. Smoothskin trailers, without exterior posts, have also been found to slip more efficiently through the air, as have disc wheels. If the fifth wheel is set right back, leaving the trailer some five or six feet behind the cab, there is a risk of turbulence, which dramatically affects the handling of the rig. To prevent this, the rig can be close coupled, or a vortex stabilizer can be fitted. This is a fin-like appliance which almost completely cancels the side-wind problem. It can be a permanent fitting, or can be supplied by the maker as a rolled up plastic sheet to be unfurled from the tractor when the trailer is attached. Another useful device is a rounded nose cone, which can be fitted to the trailer front.

Many manufacturers, conscious of the growing need for conservation, have tried to fight the fuel problem at its source – the engine. Most of them have developed

economy engines, and many other existing designs have been modified in an attempt to shave cents off the heavy gas bills. High gear haulers, who say they are unable to use top gear within the speed limit, can detune the engines by changing injectors, or making adjustments to the fuel pumps. The larger engines are not necessarily precluded from economy attempts, for a small engine running flat out can use as much fuel as a big one running at lower revs.

The automatic, or 'clutch', fan is one energy-saving package really catching on with operators. Its only purpose is to cool the engine. However, for at least 90 per cent of normal running time, the engine will not need to be cooled. A thermostat cuts off the fan when it is not needed and this increases the power conveyed to the drive train. An engine fitted with an automatic fan can be governed to run at lower revs, and give the same horse power.

The type of transmission is still very much a matter of driver preference, although the trucker should bear in mind that research and testing have proved that automatic transmissions are just as economical as manuals and they will, of course, cut down on his workload in the cab. The tires are the vehicle's only contact with the road and it is, therefore, vital that the best ones are fitted. Radials represent a real economy here, for they make firmer contact with the road, and consequently slip less and offer less

resistance. They are stronger and last longer than the cross-ply products.

Although several manufacturers have now developed what they proudly boast are energy-saving vehicles, this is not much help to those operators who are not in a financial position to trade in their rigs for some years. Indeed, it makes more economic sense to ensure that the existing rig lasts as long as possible. If an operator has a tractor with a good new, or rebuilt, engine, transmission and rear axle, most makers can offer him a package to turn his power train into a brand new rig. These packages are known as glider kits and they can save up to half of the cost of a new rig. A glider is a new cab, axle and suspension, and chassis frame. There will, of course, be a major rebuild, with used components and steep labor charges, but it is well worth it to come away with a 50 per cent saving. The conversion can be completed in a matter of weeks.

Gliders have been around for some time, but sales have only recently taken a big jump. If a young prospective trucker buys himself a beat up or wrecked old White Cabover, for example, he can have it kitted out as anything that takes his fancy, from a Peterbilt Conventional to a Mack Cruiseliner. Tag axles can be added, or cut off, and wheelbases can be altered; in fact, just about anything can be done with a pile of junk, a glider kit and a couple of mechanics who know their business. Kits usually come complete with wiring, gauges, hoses, radiator, mirrors, and lights, in addition to tanks and exhaust stacks – all the trappings of a spanking new rig.

It is likely that even greater importance will be attached to the role of the truck as it continues to dominate the world-wide surface transport of freight. Certainly the the last few years have seen a truly impressive program of development and design. There have been technological spin-offs from the aircraft, electronic, aerospace and arms industries, in addition to the contribution made by mechanical science. Trucking has also benefitted from the increased production generated at home by the tragedy of various wars being fought overseas. Many advances have been made in all

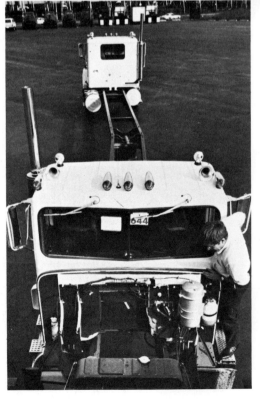

Glider kits (top) are offered by most manufacturers as a cheap way to buy a new truck. International joined these two together as a publicity gimmick. Any old truck can be turned into a Mack Cruiseliner (right).

areas of automotive and truck design, most of which have come about as a result of building war machinery.

Surprisingly, the turbine engine has not yet shown up in general production. However, the last 20 years have seen a consistent program of development of turbines for use as automotive power plants. Such immediate advantages as weight-saving and reduction of smoke emission were obvious. In 1952, Kenworth began testing a Boeing turbine which weighed in at a mere 200lbs. In addition to its light weight and smooth, almost silent, running, the motor provided such efficient power braking that wheel brakes were hardly necessary at all.

Allison has also tested its own road

Futuristic design from the movie industry (below) is more fantastic than the experimental Chevy, which did feature retractable lights (right and opposite).

turbine, in a Peterbilt Cabover on West Coast runs. This engine, although weighing 1,000lbs less than the equivalent diesel, is rated at about 280hp. Unfortunately, such beasts are thirsty for the very juice that everyone is most concerned to conserve. Difficulties such as this will delay the full-scale introduction of turbine as a revolutionary power on the roads.

Other types of motive power are, obviously, under consideration by those corporations with the foresight, and the cash, to do so. Ford have been testing rotary diesel engines, although early

The experimental Ford featured single balloon tires, but had a much higher profile than the Chevrolet.

gasoline rotaries did not realize their full potential. The gasoline and diesel engines of today are all the tried and true descendants of the primitive engines which launched the age of the auto. Although the facilities available to modern engineering make those early days look positively prehistoric, the task of designing the power plants which will take the industry into the next century is considerably more exacting.

One obvious factor to expect in futuristic truck design is aerodynamics. Trucks generally are adopting cleaner, more rounded lines. However, while there must be thousands of new design concepts already off the drawing boards, it should be expected that movement to space age tractors will be slow and subtle. The GMC Astro and the lookalike Chevrolet which have aerodynamically designed cabs, are the first really modernistic models to come out of Detroit. The thinking behind both was a good deal less than earth-shattering, but other manufacturers have taken their time in following.

Windshields are, at last, being made deeper and wider. New conventionals from International, White and GMC are looking smoother than the traditional Petes and KWs, and it is likely that future long-noses will look even sleeker. Marker lights and horns will be recessed and most of the beloved chrome features might well disappear altogether. Auto-

Marmon Trucks (right) are the 'rare breed' from Texas. The name derives from the old Marmon-Herrington marque. This small truck-maker has a square-cut 1970s look which contrasts with the style of marques like Chevy (facing page).

The experimental, wedge-shaped truck (above) is a long way from the latest double deck KW (right) although the extra high cab roof does deflect wind. The KW comes with double bunk, but can be converted to a high-ceiling cabin.

mobile styling is sure to have a great impact, particularly in conventionals which could easily begin to look like jumbo-size limousines.

In 1974, Kenworth unveiled their double deck sleeper cabs in conventional and cabover versions. With headroom for a six-footer or double stacked bunks, these were bound to find favor with the independents. The cab roof slopes up behind the driver's head and, while providing room inside, also acts as an air deflector.

Present day design thinking appears to have reached its limits and a completely new approach is obviously overdue. Wedge-shaped tractors looking something like jet planes have actually been built and tested, and ideas for a unified tractor–semi-trailer rig have been put forward.

However, one of the major factors in advanced styling is likely to be simple public relations. In Europe where there is, admittedly, less room for road vehicles, the heavy trucks have come in for fierce criticism from environmentalists. The problem is not so much noise and smoke, but the destruction or undermining of foundations in small towns where

Mack sell many trucks overseas (right) but they are competing against Mercedes, whose designers favor a low profile (above).

buildings are of historical interest. The recent upsurge in heavy trucking has provoked an emotional and powerful response in many quarters.

Mercedes Benz, still the leaders in many areas of automotive thinking, discovered in tests for a new model that vehicles which look big and brutal – the sort which drivers would classify as 'a tough-looking rig' – provoked a particularly hostile response from anti-truck quarters. Consequently, their new range for the mid-Seventies was less obtrusive. While actually increasing the internal dimensions, they managed to lower the cab and make the whole thing look smaller. With a deep sloping back windshield, the driver appears to be in a less dominant position. By dispensing with the rugged radiator grill, they completed the illusion: a truck which could gross up to 40 metric tons, and yet look as innocent as a mere middleweight city delivery outfit.

Truckers' Talk

A Glossary of terms

A

A-Car Truck made by Autocar
Advertising Lights and markings on a police car
Agitator body Concrete mixer
Anchors Brakes
Aviator Speeding driver

B

Back door (CB) Last vehicle in a convoy
Back 'em up Slow down
Balloon freight Lightweight freight
Bareback Tractor without semi-trailer
Bean hauler Vegetable or fruit hauler
Bear Policeman
Beat the Bushes First vehicle in convoy draws police out of hiding (see Shake the Leaves)
Big Hat State Trooper
Binders Brakes, or truck made by International Harvester. (Corn) Binder
Blind side Inside or right-hand side of truck
Blow the doors off Pass someone on the highway
Bobtail Either a straight truck or tractor without trailer
Bodacious Good signal, clear transmission over CB
Bogey Assembly of two or more axles
Boomers Binding devices used to tighten chains around load
Bone-box Ambulance
Bottom dumps Trailer which is unloaded through gates in the floor

Boulevard The highway, open road, or specifically the Interstate
Breaker (one nine) CB code for 'I want to talk' (on channel 19)
Brownie box Auxiliary transmission
Bucket-mouth (CB) Person who swears into his radio mic
Buddey seat Passenger or co-driver's seat
Buffalo Male hitchhiker
Bull hauler Driver of a cattle truck
Bumble Bee A two-cycle engine
Bumper Lane The outside (fast) lane
Bushel Half a ton. A twenty-ton load is 40 bushels

C

Cabover Flat-front truck, ie Cab Over Engine. Also known as COE
Cackle Crate Truck used to haul live poultry
Camera Police radar unit
Cement mixer Truck with noisy engine or transmission
Clean bore Tanker body with one undivided compartment
Chain-drive wallet One that is fixed to the belt by a chain and worn in the back pocket
Chicken coop Weigh station
Clean CB code for no cops in sight
Colorado Coolade Beer (particularly Coors)
Come-a-long Cummins diesel engine
Come On (CB) Go as fast as you like
Come back (CB) Please reply
Comic books Driver's log books
Conventional Long-nose truck
County Mounty County sheriff or deputy
Creeper gear Lowest gear in the box

Cowboy used by oldtimers to refer to a reckless driver

D

Dead-heading Running without a load (usually towards home base)
Detroit Vibrator GMC truck
Ditch light Spotlight aimed at shoulder of the road
Dock-walloper Loader or freight handler at a terminal
Dog Underpowered or worn-out truck
Doghouse Engine-cover inside a cabover tractor
Do it to it (CB) Put the hammer down
Donut Truck tire
Double bottoms Two trailers or set of doubles
Double-breasted Yamahammer Detroit diesel. (V design two-cycle engine)
Dromedary Long wheelbase tractor with load space in front of fifth wheel
Drop it on the nose Uncouple a tractor without lowering the trailer landing-gear
Duals Two tires mounted together, as used on all axles except the front
Dusting Driving with wheels on the shoulder to throw up dust
Dynamite the brakes Emergency stop using all brake systems

E

Ears CB Antennas
Eatum up Roadside restaurant or diner
Eighteen-wheeler Any tractor-trailer truck

Exempt commodities Goods which are not covered by ICC regulations, and which can be hauled by independents

F

Fat load Overweight
Feed the bears Collect a ticket
Fifth wheel A round plate at rear of tractor to which a pin on the semi-trailer is connected
Five Five 55 mph speed limit
Fix Or Repair Daily Ford truck
Flatbed Truck or trailer without sides or top covering
Flip-flop (CB) Return trip
Floats Large single tires in place of duals
Four-banger Four cylinder engine
Four by four Four-speed transmission with four-speed auxiliary giving 16 forward gears
Four ten Emphatic variation on 10-4 (CB code)
Four wheeler Passenger car
Front door First vehicle in convoy
Fruitliner Freightliner truck

G

Garbage hauler Produce hauler
Gear Bonger Driver who grinds gears when shifting
Gear Jammer Originally as Bonger, but now means anyone who drives a truck
Georgia Overdrive Neutral gear used on a down grade (also Mexican or Midnight Overdrive)
Glad hands Connections for air lines between tractor and trailer
Goat 'n Shoat jockey Driver of a livestock truck
Go-Go Girls Pigs or hogs which jump around in the trailer
Going home hole Top gear
Grab one Shift into lower gear going up hill
Grass Side of the road
Green stamps (CB) Money to pay speeding tickets
Green stamp road Toll road
Gypsy An independent trucker without a regular run

H

Hammer down Drive fast or highball
Handle Slang name for CB identification
Headache rack Bulkhead at rear of cab to protect it from shifting loads
Hood-lifter Garage mechanic
Hopper Truck or trailer body with bottom opening doors (see bottom dump)
Horses Horsepower of engine
Hot load Cargo that needs to be delivered quickly
Hundred-mile coffee A strong brew as served at truck stops
Hundred-dollar hole top gear

I

In the grass Parked beside the road
Iron-lunger A small engine of 250 hp or less

J

Jackknife Incident when a semi slides out of control the trailer swings round and hits the tractor
Japanese Freightliner A truck made by White (originally cheaper than most)
Jimmy GMC truck
Jump the pin Miss the fifth wheel pin when coupling tractor to trailer

K

Keep the rubber side down and the shiny side up (CB) Drive safely (there are many variations of this phrase)
Kick down Downshift
Kick it back (CB) Your turn to speak please reply
Kidney-buster Rough riding truck
Kitty Kat Caterpillar diesel engine
KW, or K-Whopper Truck made by Kenworth

L

Landing gear Legs which support the semi-trailer when it is not coupled to the tractor
Lay on air Apply the brakes
Lie sheet Log-book
Loaded with sailboat fuel, or post holes Running empty
Lowboy Trailer for hauling extra heavy loads such as machinery

M

Maniac Mechanic
May pop Suspect or slick tire
Mexican Overdrive See Georgia
Milk run Easy journey
Montfort Lane Fast lane, named after Montfort Line coast-to-coast meat haulers
Mule Tractor used for shunting trailers in yard

N

Negatory (CB) Negative reply
Nose dive Trailer tipped forward on its nose

O

Oakie-blower Scoop on air-intake to force air into engine and increase power
On the ground Out of the vehicle
On the side Parked up or pulled over
On rubber Rolling

P

P and D's Pick-up and deliveries
Pajama wagon Sleeper cab tractor
Pavement princess Truck-stop hooker
Peanut wagon Small tractor pulling a large trailer
Pete or Peter Car Truck made by Peterbilt

Peg leg, tandem Tractor with only one axle driven

Pharmaceuticals Amphetamines

Pickum-up truck Pick-up or light truck

Picture taker (CB) Bear using his radar

Piggyback Trailers carried on railroad flat cars

Pigtail Electrical cable from tractor to trailer

Pike Turnpike

Plain wrapper (CB) Unmarked police car

Portable parking lot Automobile transporter

Portable pipeline Tanker truck

Pour on Coal Step on the gas

Pump jockey Attendant at truck stop

Pumpkin Flat tire

Pup Short semi-trailer used with a dolly and towed behind a tractor trailer

Pussy power Caterpillar engine

Put on the air Hit the brakes

Put on the iron Fix snow chains

Put the good numbers on you (CB) Best regards, good luck

Put the pedal to the metal (CB) Put the hammer down, go as fast as you like

R

Radar alley Interstate 90 Ohio, the danger state for speeding truckers

Radidio CB

Rags Bad tires

Rag top Open-top trailer covered with a tarpaulin

Rake the leaves (CB) Back door or last vehicle in a convoy

Ratchet-jaw A non-stop talker who monopolises the CB

Rest em up Roadside rest area

Reefer Refrigerated trailer or truck

Rig Any truck, or sometimes refers to a CB radio

Roach Coach Furniture-moving van

Rocking chair (CB) Vehicle which is anywhere in the middle of a convoy

Roger (CB) Same as 10-4, O.K., message received

Roller-skate Small car

S

Saddle tank Fuel tanks located on each side of a tractor

Second driver Amphetamine, or speed pill

Semi Tractor-trailer rig where the front of the semi-trailer is coupled to the tractor and has no front axle of its own

Shake the leaves (CB) See beat the bushes

Set it down Stop quickly

Shake the lights Blink or flash headlights as a warning signal

Sheep-herder Driver of questionable ability

Shopping cart Grocery truck

Sick horse A truck in a poor state of mechanical repair

Six-banger Six cylinder engine

Six-wheeler Car towing a trailer, or a straight truck with two axles

Skinnie axle Single axle trailer

Slip-a-matic Automatic transmission

Smokey Bear. Cop or State Trooper, so called because the Big Hats some Troopers wear are similar to the Smokey Bear ranger hats

Smokestack Vertical exhaust pipe at side of cab

Spy in the sky (CB) or **Bear in the air** Police in helicopters or planes

Spin out Lose traction on slippery road

Split shift Simultaneous shifting of gears in main and auxiliary boxes

Spot the body Park the trailer

Stack See smokestack

Stake body Truck or trailer with removable side stakes

Strip her Unload the trailer

Suicide jockey One who hauls explosives or dangerous loads

Suicide box Sleeper compartment

Super slab See boulevard

Swamper Driver's helper, or 'shotgun rider'

Swindle sheet ICC permit for Interstate hauling

T

Tailgating Driving too close to the vehicle in front

Tandem Two axles, either on tractor or trailer

Tattle tale Tachograph device which records hours and speeds driven

Thermos bottle Tank trailer

Tijuana taxi Well-marked police car

Tooling down the highway Driving along at a legal speed

Triples Set of three trailers

Trolley brake A hand valve used to operate trailer brakes only

Truck 'em up stop (CB) Truck stop

Twin screw A truck with two rear axles both driven by the engine

Twinkle Star Transtar truck, built by International

W

Wall to wall bears High concentration of police

Wide Spread Trailer axles which are more than eight feet apart

We gone (CB) Stopping transmission

West Coasts Side mirrors, deep and flat

West Coast turnaround See second driver

Woodchuck Company driver with low seniority

X

XYL Ex young lady or wife. Also XYM, husband

Y

Yardbird Driver who moves vehicles around yard

Yard mule Small tractor used to moved semi-trailers around yard

Z

Zephyr haul Shipment of light-weight cargo

Zoo Police headquarters

THE TRUCK MANUFACTURERS
OF THE UNITED STATES

Autocar Trucks,
930 East Lincoln Highway,
Exton, Pennsylvania 19341.

Brockway Motor Trucks,
106 Central Avenue,
Cortland, New York 13045.

Chevrolet Motor Division,
General Motors Corp.,
3044 West Grand Boulevard,
Detroit, Michigan 48202.

FWD Corp.,
105 East 12th St.,
Cliftonville, Wisconsin 54929.

Ford Motor Company,

Dearborn, Michigan 48121.

Freightliner Corp.,
4747 North Channel Avenue,
Portland, Oregon 97217.

GMC Truck and Coach,
General Motors Corp.,
660 South Blvd. East
Pontiac, Michigan 48053.

Hendrickson Mfg. Co.,
8001 West 47th St.,
Lyons, Illinois 60534.

International Trucks,
International Harvester Co.,
401 North Michigan Ave.,
Chicago, Illinois 60611.

Kenworth Truck Co.,
8801 East Marginal Way,
P.O. Box 80222,
Seattle, Washington 98108.

Mack Trucks,
Box M,
Allentown, Pennsylvania 18105

Marmon Motor Company,
P.O. Box 5175,
Dallas, Texas 75222.

Oshkosh Truck Corp.,
2300 Oregon St.,
Oshkosh, Wisconsin 54901.

Peterbilt Motors Co.,
38801 Cherry St.,
P.O. Box 404,
Newark, California 94560.

White Trucks,
842 East 79th St.,
Cleveland, Ohio 44101.

ORIGINAL
PHOTOGRAPHY BY

John Mason: endpapers, pages 6, 14, 15, 16, 19, 20/21, 22, 23, 24, 25, 28/29 (top), 54, 56, 57, 58, 60/61 (top), 64/65, 68/69, 72/73, 74, 83, 85, 89, 92, 93, 98, 101, 102, 103 (top), 104/104, 107 (top), 109, 110, 114, 115, 117 (bottom), 120/121, 163, 164, 166, 168/169, 170, 175, 179 (bottom), 187.

Graeme Ewens: pages 11, 13, 79, 80, 82, 84, 86, 87, 90, 91, 100, 103 (bottom), 106, 107 (bottom), 108, 112/113, 117 (top), 118, 119, 120, 121 (top), 165 (bottom), 171.

Michael Ellis: pages 2, 8/9, 177.

Andrew Morland: pages 4, 162.

Pat Kennett: pages 62/63, 186.

Malcolm Russell: page 188 (top).

Additional material supplied by:
American Trucking Associations Inc. (pages 10, 12, 18, 30, 34, 35, 36/37, 38/39, 40/41, 44, 47, 94, 96, 97, 180, 181, 182, 183). Bryan Chalker, Jerry Malone, GMC Trucks, Ford Motor Co, Freightliner Corp., Mack Trucks, White Motor Corp., Transamerican Press, Virginia Dept. of Highways and Transportation, International Trucks, Kenworth Truck Co.

Columbia Pictures, Paramount Pictures, Anthony Balch, Universal Pictures, Warner Bros Inc, MGM Inc

ACKNOWLEDGEMENTS

The author would like to acknowledge the assistance of the following, without whose co-operation the book could not have been written: Loyd W. Cogburn, Don Barrett, Theo Burks, Independent Truckers Association, American Trucking Associations Inc., W. W. Johnson, Dell Roll, Bryan Chalker, Gib Grace, 'Colonel Eagle', 'Four by Four', 'Going Broke', Nick Baldwin, California Highway Patrol.